IQ AND APTITUDE TESTS

www.How2Become.com

Get more products for passing
any type of test or interview at:

www.how2become.com

As part of this product you have also
received **FREE** access to online tests
that will help you to pass abstract
reasoning tests

To gain access, simply go to:

www.PsychometricTestsOnline.co.uk

More psychometric testing books and online tests by How2Become.com

- Numerical reasoning tests

- Spatial reasoning tests

- Verbal reasoning tests

- Quantitative reasoning tests

- QTS numerical tests

- Abstract reasoning tests

- GCSE mathematics

- 11+ test questions

- Psychometric tests

- Speed, distance and time tests

- Fuel calculation tests

- Armed force tests

All of the above products and online tests are now available via our website:

www.How2become.com

Orders: Please contact How2become Ltd, Suite 3, 50 Churchill Square Business Centre, Kings Hill, Kent ME19 4YU. You can also order via the e mail address info@how2become.co.uk.

ISBN: 9781910202760

First published in 2014 by How2Become Ltd

Typeset for How2become Ltd by Anton Pshinka.

Printed in Great Britain for How2become Ltd by CMP

CONTENTS

INTRODUCTION TO YOUR GUIDE

Dear Sir/Madam,

Welcome to your new guide, IQ and Aptitude Tests. This guide contains lots of sample test questions that are appropriate for anyone who is required to take a career-related IQ and Aptitude test. The key to success in any career or job-related assessment is to try your hardest to get 100% correct answers in the test that you are undertaking. If you aim for 100% in your preparation, then you are far more likely to achieve the trade or career that you want. We have deliberately supplied you with lots of sample questions to assist you. It is crucial that when you get a question wrong, you take the time to find out why you got it wrong. Understanding the question is very important.

Finally, if you want to try out more tests that will prepare you for your assessment then we offer a wide range of products to assist you at **www.how2become.com.**

Good luck and best wishes,

The How2become team

PREFACE BY AUTHOR RICHARD MCMUNN

It's probably important that I start off by explaining a little bit about myself, my background, and also why I'm suitably qualified to help you prepare for your test.

At the time of writing I am 42 years old and live in Tunbridge Wells, Kent. I left school at the usual age of 16 and joined the Royal Navy, serving on-board HMS Invincible as part of 800 Naval Air Squadron which formed part of the Fleet Air Arm. There I was, at the age of 16, travelling the world and working as an engineer on Sea Harrier jets! It was fantastic and I loved every minute of it. After four years I left the Royal Navy and joined Kent Fire and Rescue Service as a firefighter.

Over the next 17 years I worked my way up through the ranks to the position of Assistant Divisional Officer. During my time in the Fire Service I spent a lot of time working as an instructor at the Fire Brigade Training Centre. I was also involved in the selection process for assessing candidates who wanted to join the job as a firefighter. Therefore, my knowledge and experience gained so far in life has been invaluable in helping people like you to pass any type of selection process. I am sure you will find this guide an invaluable resource during your preparation for your assessment.

I have always been fortunate in the fact that I persevere at everything I do. I've understood that if I keep working hard in life then I will always be successful; or I will achieve whatever it is that I want to achieve. This is an important lesson that I want you to take on-board straight away. If you work hard and persevere, then success will come your way. It is also very important that you believe in your own abilities. It does not matter if you have no qualifications. It does not matter if you are currently weak in the area of IQ and aptitude tests or psychometric testing. What does matter is self-belief, self-discipline and a genuine desire to improve and become successful.

Finally, as part of this product I want to give you FREE access to online tests that will help you to pass your IQ and aptitude test. To gain access, simply go to:

www.PsychometricTestsOnline.co.uk

Best wishes,

Richard McMunn

Richard McMunn

DISCLAIMER

Every effort has been made to ensure that the information contained within this guide is accurate at the time of publication. How2become Ltd are not responsible for anyone failing any part of any selection process as a result of the information contained within this guide. How2become Ltd and their authors cannot accept any responsibility for any errors or omissions within this guide, however caused. No responsibility for loss or damage occasioned by any person acting, or refraining from action, as a result of the material in this publication can be accepted by How2become Ltd.

The information within this guide does not represent the views of any third party service or organisation.

ABOUT IQ AND APTITUDE TESTS

IQ and Aptitude tests are an important element of a psychometric test. The tests are designed to measure trait intelligence (IQ) and cognitive ability, which is indicated by your efficiency in information processing. Whilst IQ and aptitude tests are designed to test your intelligence, you can actually practice for them, which in turn has been proven to increase scores.

The tests are predominantly used to determine if you are fit for a certain job. The tests used by an employer to assess candidates for a role will be indicative of the role they are required to perform. For example, a bank would most probably use numerical and data interpretation tests whilst assessing bank cashier positions, whilst roles within the aviation industry would utilise spatial and abstract reasoning as part of their assessment. Therefore, it is important that you find out the types of test question you are going to encounter during your particular assessment, and then practice as many as possible under timed conditions in the days and weeks leading up to your test. You can usually find out the types of test question you will be required to undertake by reading the pre-test materials sent by the test centre, or alternatively contacting the test centre directly and asking them for this information.

Within this guide we have provided nine individual test sections which cover the following areas:

- Mental arithmetic, sections 1 and 2
- Ratios
- Fractions
- Number sequence
- Spatial aptitude
- Grammar and punctuation
- General verbal aptitude
- Abstract and diagrammatic reasoning

Before we provide you with a host of sample test questions and answers, let's take a look at some of the more common questions we get asked by people preparing for IQ and aptitude tests.

How long are the tests?

The time that you will be provided to sit the test will very much depend on the role you are applying for. However, to give you an idea, the tests that form part of the UK clinical aptitude test last for a maximum of 14 minutes, during which time the candidate has to answer 55 questions. The tests are designed so that it is very difficult to complete them. Whilst the assessor or test centre are looking for you to complete as many test questions as possible, they are also looking for you to get the questions you have answered, correct. Therefore, during your preparation you must concentrate on speed as well as accuracy.

What if there are too many questions and I don't have the time to finish them all?

In the majority of IQ and aptitude tests you are not expected to answer all of the questions. When you turn over the test paper, or when you start your online test, you may see that the total number of questions in the test is excessive for the amount of time you are given to answer them. If this is the case, do not panic; you are not expected to finish the test. These tests are usually designed so that it is very difficult to complete all of the questions. The key to remember is that you must try to answer as many questions as possible, but you should also aim for accuracy. Some test centres will deduct marks for incorrect answers or guessing; therefore, the key to passing the tests is to aim for speed as well as accuracy!

What if my test is online?

If you are required to undertake your test online then you will normally be allowed to decide where and when you take it. Most employers will send you a link to access the online test and give you a timescale in which to complete it. You should, therefore, think carefully about what time is best suited for you to take the test.

Do you perform better in the morning, or do you work better in the evening? You should also think carefully about where you are going to take the test; for example, if you are taking the test at home, are your family aware of this and will they leave you free from distraction? It is advisable that you plan and prepare for your online test well in advance of taking it. Don't forget to think of important factors such as making sure you have a good internet connection and also that your phone is turned off during the test.

You should also take the test on a computer which you are comfortable with and familiar with. Make sure the screen is large enough and also make sure there are charged batteries in the mouse, if you are using a wireless one. Also, make sure you have everything you need before you take your test, such as a calculator, a pencil, some drinking water and plenty of blank paper to take notes. Finally, be sure to go to the toilet before you take your IQ and aptitude test as some of the tests can take longer than an hour!

Will I be able to use a calculator during the test?

Dependent on the level of difficulty of the test, you may or may not be permitted to use a calculator. Having said that, for online tests you will normally be permitted to use your own calculator. If this is the case for your particular test, be sure to use one that you are use to, or one which you have been practicing with for some time prior to the test. Remember, every second counts during the test – the last thing you want to be doing is learning how to use the calculator in the middle of the test!

Make sure you choose one with which you are familiar; perhaps that old one you've had since your GCSEs for example. The time pressure during psychometric tests is intense, so if you can save a few vital seconds by not having to look down at your calculator to find where the divide button is, then you are giving yourself the best possible chance to perform well.

Online calculators are becoming increasingly common during online tests – these are the type of calculator which appear on the screen, usually in the bottom right hand corner, during the test. If you are required to use an online calculator it will normally be of a simple format, very much like the old Casio calculators most of us used at school.

If your test is conducted at an assessment centre or at the employer's office you will probably have to use the calculator they supply you. This is usually done to ensure fairness and consistency amongst the test takers.

What is the pass mark for my test?

Many people are interested in the pass mark for their forthcoming assessment. The truth is that many test administrators will score and assess candidates based on an average score for the entire group of applicants. Therefore, you should not become overly concerned about reaching an actual pass mark of say 70%, but instead concentrate on answering as many questions in an accurate manner.

Who creates the test questions?

The employer, who you are required to take a test for, will usually outsource the creation of the IQ and aptitude test. This effectively means you are able to obtain sample test questions direct from the test creator which will be similar to the test questions you will encounter during the real test.

There are a number of aptitude test publishers in existence and each of them has a slightly different style and test format. Within the sample testing literature, or within the online link you are provided with to practice the tests, will be clues as to which test creator is behind the IQ and aptitude test you are required to sit. Once you find out which test creator it is who has created the test for the employer, go direct to their website and look for further additional practice questions. You may also be able to find out additional important information about the test you are taking, such as whether they deduct marks for incorrect answers (negative marking) or even the time limit for your particular test.

To give you an idea of the types of company that are commonly used during test creation, here is a list of companies along with their dedicated website:

SHL – www.shl.com

Saville Consulting - www.savilleconsulting.com

TalentQ - www.talentqgroup.com

Cubiks - www.cubiks.com

Criterion Partnership - www.criterionpartnership.co.uk

Kenexa - www.psl.com

Why do most people fail the tests?

One of the more common reasons why people fail their test is because they do not read the question. It is vitally important you read the questions carefully, and also take the time to listen to the brief prior to the test.

You should particularly pay attention to how you are required to answer the questions. Are you required to circle the right answer, strike it through, shade a box of your answer option, or write your answer option on a separate answer book? Don't forget, if you pass a question you must make sure you leave a gap on the answer sheet, otherwise ALL of your proceeding answers will be wrong!

It is a good idea to pay attention to the time limit for the test. For example, if there are 40 questions in the test and you have 10 minutes to complete them, this gives you just 15 seconds per question on average. If you get stuck on a particular question, move on and come back to it later if you have time, but don't forget to leave a space on the answer sheet.

Is it acceptable for me to guess if I find I am running out of time?

My advice is to avoid wild-guessing at all costs! Remember, some test centres will deduct marks for incorrect answers. Having said that, it is certainly worth learning the skill of what I call 'best-guessing'. Best-guessing can only be utilised during multiple-choice type questions. It basically requires you to eliminate quickly any glaringly incorrect answer options. This technique, which I used to use during my early days in the Fire service whilst taking tests for promotion, is a useful one if you find you are short of time and you feel you have not answered enough questions to gain high marks. For example if you can easily see that an answer should be within a specific range, or it needs to have certain units, you should be able to discount two or three of the answer options quickly, which then leaves you with a 50:50 chance of getting the answer correct.

Are there any further tips you can offer me to help me prepare fully for my tests?

- Whilst it is important to find out the types of questions you will be required to undertake during the real test, I do also feel that variety during practice will help you to increase your scores. I recommend that you attempt a variety of different test questions, such as general psychometric tests, numerical reasoning, verbal reasoning, abstract reasoning, spatial aptitude, fault analysis and mechanical reasoning etc. This will undoubtedly improve your overall ability to pass the IQ and aptitude test that you are required to undertake. If you go to the free tests at www.PsychometricTestsOnline.co.uk then you will be able to try all of these free of charge. I would also recommend you obtain my other psychometric testing booklets from either Amazon or through How2Become.com as these books are also great additional preparation for an IQ and aptitude test.

- Confidence is an important part of test preparation. Have you ever sat a timed test and your mind goes blank? This is because your mind is focused on negative thoughts and your belief that you will fail the test. If you practice plenty of test questions under timed conditions then your confidence will grow. If your confidence is at its peak at the commencement of the test then there is no doubt that you will actually look forward to sitting it, as opposed to being fearful of the outcome.

- Whilst this is a very basic tip that may appear obvious, many people neglect to follow it. Make sure that you get a good night's sleep the night before your test or assessment. Research has shown that those people who have regular 'good' sleep are far more likely to concentrate better during IQ and aptitude tests.

- Aim for SPEED as well as ACCURACY. Many test centres want to see how quickly you can work, but they also want to see how accurate your work is, too. Therefore, when tackling the tests you must work as quickly as you can without sacrificing accuracy. Most tests are designed so that you do no finish them and you will most probably lose marks for incorrect answers.

- You are what you eat! In the week prior to the test eat and drink healthily. Avoid cigarettes, alcohol and food with high fat content. The reason for this is that all of these will make you feel sluggish and you will not perform at your peak. On the morning of your assessment eat a healthy breakfast such as porridge and a banana.

- Drink plenty of water, always!

- If you have any special needs that need to be catered for ensure you inform the assessment centre staff prior to the assessment day. I have met people in the past who are fearful of telling the assessment staff that they are dyslexic. You will not be treated negatively; in fact the exact opposite. They will give you extra time in the tests which can only work in your favour.

Now that I have provided you with a number of important tips, take the time to work through the nine different sample test sections that are contained within the guide.

You will need a stopwatch in order to assess your performance against the time constraints for each test.

With regards to using a calculator during the sample tests, please try to tackle them without one as this will help to improve your confidence and ability during the real test.

IQ & APTITUDE TEST
SECTION 1
(Mental arithmetic)

In IQ & Aptitude Test section 1 there are 50 questions and you have just 20 minutes to answer them

IQ AND APTITUDE TEST SECTION 1

Q1. What is 8 multiplied by 6?

Answer

Q2. What is 4 multiplied by 7?

Answer

Q3. What is 6 multiplied by 9?

Answer

Q4. What is 9 multiplied by 9?

Answer

Q5. What is 8 multiplied by 7?

Answer

Q6. What is 12 multiplied by 6?

Answer

Q7. What is 13 multiplied by 7?

Answer

Q8. What is 12 multiplied by 12?

Answer

Q9. What is 15 multiplied by 6?

Answer

Q10. What is 20 multiplied by 20?

Answer

Q11. What is 50% of 250?

Answer

Q12. What is 60% of 500?

Answer

Q13. What is 40% of 300?

Answer

Q14. What is 70% of 800?

Answer

Q15. What is 45% of 120?

Answer

Q16. What is 65% of 210?

Answer

Q17. What is 32% of 98?

Answer

Q18. What is 44% of 200?

Answer

Q19. What is 56% of 170?

Answer

Q20. What is 80% of 900?

Answer

Q21. What is 4/5 of 70?

Answer

Q22. What is 3/4 of 180?

Answer

Q23. What is 2/6 of 300?

Answer

Q24. What is 5/8 of 64?

Answer

Q25. What is 7/8 of 136?

Answer

Q26. What is 9/13 of 208?

Answer

Q27. What is 1/4 of 800?

Answer

Q28. What is 2/3 of 660?

Answer

Q29. What is 4/7 of 154?

Answer

Q30. What is 2/5 of 412?

Answer

Q31. Multiply 11 by 5 and then divide by 5

Answer [   ]

Q32. Multiply 6 by 7 and then divide by 3

Answer [   ]

Q33. Multiply 8 by 9 and then divide it by 2

Answer [   ]

Q34. Divide 24 by 3 and then multiply it by 4

Answer [   ]

Q35. Divide 49 by 7 and then multiply it by 12

Answer [   ]

Q36. Subtract 12 from 84 and then divide it by 4

Answer [   ]

Q37. Subtract 14 from 92 and then multiply it by 2

Answer [   ]

Q38. Multiply 6 by 4 and then divide it by 3

Answer [   ]

Q39. Divide 56 by 7 and then subtract it by 5

Answer [   ]

Q40. Multiply 6 by 6 and then multiply it by 4

Answer [   ]

Q41. What is 13 multiplied by 3?

Answer [   ]

Q42. What is 15 multiplied by 5?

Answer [   ]

Q43. What is 20 multiplied by 120?

Answer

Q44. What is 30% of 400?

Answer

Q45. What is 5% of 150?

Answer

Q46. What is 95% of 60?

Answer

Q47. What is 9/11 of 88?

Answer

Q48. What is 2/7 of 490?

Answer

Q49. Multiply 8 by 3 and then multiply it by 3

Answer

Q50. Divide 120 by 4 and then multiply it by 5

Answer

Please now check your answers carefully before moving onto the next section of the guide.

ANSWERS TO IQ AND APTITUDE TEST SECTION 1

Q1. 48

Q2. 28

Q3. 54

Q4. 81

Q5. 56

Q6. 72

Q7. 91

Q8. 144

Q9. 90

Q10. 400

Q11. 125

Q12. 300

Q13. 120

Q14. 560

Q15. 54

Q16. 136.5

Q17. 31.36

Q18. 88

Q19. 95.2

Q20. 720

Q21. 56

Q22. 135

Q23. 100

Q24. 40

Q25. 119

Q26. 144

Q27. 200

Q28. 440

Q29. 88

Q30. 164.8

Q31. 11

Q32. 14

Q33. 36

Q34. 32

Q35. 84

Q36. 18

Q37. 156

Q38. 8

Q39. 3

Q40. 144

Q41. 39

Q42. 75

Q43. 2400

Q44. 120

Q45. 7.5

Q46. 57

Q47. 72

Q48. 140

Q49. 72

Q50. 150

Now move onto the next section of the guide.

IQ & APTITUDE TEST
SECTION 2
(Mental arithmetic)

*In IQ & Aptitude Test section 2 there are 50 questions
and you have just 20 minutes to answer them*

IQ AND APTITUDE TEST SECTION 2

Q1. What is 10% of 140 plus 18?

Answer [   ]

Q2. What is 20% of 155 minus 8?

Answer [   ]

Q3. What is 45% of 210 multiplied by 10?

Answer [   ]

Q4. What is 50% of 500 divided by 5?

Answer [   ]

Q5. What is 60% of 340 minus 27?

Answer [   ]

Q6. What is 80% of 600 multiplied by 12?

Answer [   ]

Q7. What is 24% of 80 minus 6?

Answer

Q8. What is 36% of 120 plus 14?

Answer

Q9. What is 58% of 700 divided by 7?

Answer

Q10. What is 9% 840 multiplied by 3?

Answer

Q11. Divide 24 by 4 and add it to 8 multiplied by 5

Answer

Q12. Multiply 8 by 12 and subtract it by 2 multiplied by 3 minus 1

Answer

Q13. Add 50 by 49 and divide it by 4 multiplied by 2 add 3

Answer

Q14. Subtract 80 from 120 and add it to 12 multiplied by 6

Answer

Q15. Divide 36 by 6 and multiply it to 40 divided by 5

Answer

Q16. Multiply 21 by 3 and subtract it from 108 multiplied by 2 minus 27

Answer

Q17. Add 150 by 210 and divide it by 3 multiplied by 3

Answer

Q18. Subtract 360 by 110 and add it to 90 divided by 6

Answer

Q19. Divide 48 by 8 and multiply it to 80 divided by 5 multiplied by 4

Answer

Q20. Multiply 37 by 4 and add it to 60 divided by 10 multiplied by 9

Answer

Q21. What is 2/5 of 40?

Answer

Q22. What is 3/7 of 49?

Answer

Q23. What is 5/8 of 256?

Answer

Q24. What is 1/8 of 128?

Answer

Q25. What is 9/12 of 288?

Answer

Q26. What is 8/13 of 195?

Answer

Q27. What is 4/5 of 130?

Answer

Q28. What is 5/7 of 147?

Answer

Q29. What is 2/3 of 660?

Answer

Q30. What is 5/6 of 780?

Answer

Q31. Add 3/4 of 108 to 2/5 of 65

Answer [   ]

Q32. Add 3/7 of 63 to 2/3 of 45

Answer [   ]

Q33. Add 3/5 of 180 to 1/4 of 120

Answer [   ]

Q34. Subtract 1/4 of 140 from 2/3 of 450

Answer [   ]

Q35. Subtract 2/6 of 360 from 4/5 of 580

Answer [   ]

Q36. Multiply 1/4 of 60 by 1/3 of 63

Answer [   ]

Q37. Subtract 1/7 of 49 from 4/6 of 72

Answer

Q38. Subtract 3/8 of 104 from 5/7 of 98

Answer

Q39. Multiply 1/2 of 22 by 1/3 of 30

Answer

Q40. Add 7/9 of 189 to 5/8 of 128

Answer

Q41. What is 45% of 590 minus 8?

Answer

Q42. What is 71% of 160 add 13?

Answer

Q43. What is 15% of 300 multiplied by 4?

Answer

Q44. Multiply 6 by 11 and add it to 5 multiplied by 4 add 15

Answer

Q45. Divide 42 by 7 and multiply it to 60 divided by 5 multiplied by 4

Answer

Q46. What is 4/7 of 735?

Answer

Q47. What is 7/8 of 168?

Answer

Q48. What is 5/9 of 288?

Answer

Q49. Add 3/4 of 408 to 2/3 of 39

Answer

Q50. Multiply 1/3 of 66 by 3/5 of 70

Answer

Please now check your answers carefully before moving onto the next section of the guide.

ANSWERS TO IQ AND APTITUDE TEST SECTION 2

Q1. 32

Q2. 23

Q3. 945

Q4. 50

Q5. 177

Q6. 5760

Q7. 13.2

Q8. 57.2

Q9. 58

Q10. 226.8

Q11. 46

Q12. 91

Q13. 9

Q14. 112

Q15. 48

Q16. 126

Q17. 40

Q18. 265

Q19. 384

Q20. 202

Q21. 16

Q22. 21

Q23. 160

Q24. 16

Q25. 216

Q26. 120

Q27. 104

Q28. 105

Q29. 440

Q30. 650

Q31. 107

Q32. 57

Q33. 138

Q34. 265

Q35. 344

Q36. 315

Q37. 41

Q38. 31

Q39. 110

Q40. 227

Q41. 257.5

Q42. 126.6

Q43. 180

Q44. 101

Q45. 288

Q46. 420

Q47. 147

Q48. 160

Q49. 332

Q50. 924

Now move onto the next section of the guide.

IQ & APTITUDE TEST
SECTION 3
(Fractions)

*In IQ & Aptitude Test section 3 there are 50 questions
and you have 50 minutes to answer them*

IQ AND APTITUDE TEST SECTION 3

Q1. 2 1/4 + 3 1/2 =

A. 4 1/4

B. 5 5/9

C. 5 3/4

D. 4 3/4

Answer

Q2. 1 3/5 + 2 3/7 =

A. 4 3/30

B. 6 1/6

C. 5

D. 4 1/35

Answer

Q3. 7 1/6 + 3 1/3 =

A. 10 2/3

B. 10 1/2

C. 10 6/3

D. 11 1/2

Answer

Q4. 3 5/8 + 4 1/8 =

A. 12 1/4

B. 6 7/8

C. 7 3/4

D. 10 1/2

Answer

Q5. 2 8/9 + 3 2/3 =

A. 5 6/9

B. 6 5/9

C. 5 10/12

D. 12 4/9

Answer

Q6. 2 3/4 + 1 5/8 =

A. 3 1/2

B. 3 2/3

C. 4 3/8

D. 4 5/8

Answer

Q7. 3 4/9 + 2 5/6 =

A. 6 5/18

B. 6 1/3

C. 5 3/5

D. 5 1/3

Answer [   ]

Q8. 1 9/10 + 4 3/5 =

A. 6 1/2

B. 5 7/10

C. 5 3/10

D. 4 1/5

Answer [   ]

Q9. 1 5/6 + 3 1/2 =

A. 2 4/4

B. 2 1/3

C. 5 1/3

D. 10/11

Answer [   ]

Q10. 2 5/6 + 3 3/4 =

A. 6 7/12

B. 7 1/12

C. 11/12

D. 10 1/2

Answer [ ]

Q11. It takes Linda 1/2 hour to get washed and changed before school. It takes her 15 minutes to go downstairs and eat her breakfast. How much time does it take Linda to be ready before school?

A. 3/4 hour

B. 1 hour

C. 1 1/4 hours

D. 2/4 hour

Answer [ ]

Q12. It takes Sam 3/4 of an hour to get ready for school and have breakfast. It takes another 3/4 of an hour on the bus to get to school. How much time does it take Sam to get ready and get to school?

A 1/2 hour

B. 1 3/4 hours

C. 1 1/2 hours

D. 2 hours

Answer [   ]

Q13. A family are on their way to the Zoo. They spend 1 1/2 hours to drive there. They spend 5 3/4 hours at the Zoo. How much time is spent driving to and from the Zoo including the hours they were there for?

A. 7 1/2 hours

B. 9 hours

C. 8 3/4 hours

D. 8 1/4 hours

Answer [   ]

Q14. Peter spends a 1/4 of an hour on stretching before his big race. He spends 1/2 an hour preparing for the race and getting ready. The race itself is 1 hour long. How much time does Peter spend in preparation and running the race?

A. 1 hour

B. 1 3/4 hours

C. 2 hours

D. 1 1/2 hours

Answer [   ]

Q15. A family are on their way to Thorpe Park. They spend 1 1/4 hours to drive there. They spend 6 1/2 hours at the Thorpe Park. How much time is spent driving to and from Thorpe Park including the hours they were there for?

A. 9 1/4 hours

B. 8 1/2 hours

C. 9 hours

D. 8 3/4 hours

Answer

Q16. A Science exam lasts 1 1/2 hours. An English exam lasts 2 hours. A Maths exam last 3/4 of an hour. How much time is spent in exams if a student were to sit all three exams?

A. 5 3/4 hours

B. 4 1/2 hours

C. 5 hours

D. 4 1/4 hours

Answer

Q17. It takes James 1 1/4 hours to get ready for work in the mornings. It takes another 3/4 of an hour to drive to his work. How much time does it take James to get ready and get to work in the mornings?

A. 2 hours

B. 2 1/2 hours

C. 2 1/4 hours

D. 1 3/4 hours

Answer [   ]

Q18. A Law exam lasts 1 3/4 hours. A History exam lasts 2 1/2 hours. A Geography exam last 2 1/4 hours. How much time is spent in exams if a student were to sit all three exams?

A. 6 3/4 hours

B. 6 1/2 hours

C. 7 hours

D. 6 1/4 hours

Answer [   ]

Q19. It takes Martin 1/2 hour to get washed and changed before school. It takes him 1/4 of an hour to go downstairs and eat breakfast. It takes him 1 1/4 hours on the bus to school. How much time does it take Martin to get ready and get to school?

A. 2 hours

B. 1 1/2 hours

C. 2 1/2 hours

D. 1 3/4 hours

Answer [   ]

Q20. Mia spends 1/2 hour preparing for her Dance audition. She spends 1/4 of an hour signing in. She waits 3/4 of an hour before it is her turn. She spends 1/4 of an hour dancing. How much time does it take to prepare and sign in and dance her audition, including the waiting time she had to wait?

A. 1 1/2 hours

B. 2 hours

C. 1 3/4 hours

D. 3 hours

Answer

Q21. Which two fractions are equivalent?

A. 3/8 and 8/3

B. 1/2 and 1/4

C. 1/4 and 3/12

D. 3/5 and 7/10

Answer

Q22. Which two fractions are equivalent?

A. 4/6 and 6/4

B. 5/4 and 10/8

C. 3/5 and 2/5

D. 4/7 and 8/7

Answer [   ]

Q23. Which two fractions are equivalent?

A. 4/5 and 9/10

B. 2/3 and 3/2

C. 15/10 and 5/5

D. 18/16 and 9/8

Answer [   ]

Q24. Which two fractions are equivalent?

A. 2/4 and 1/2

B. 3/4 and 4/3

C. 5/9 and 10/20

D. 6/7 and 12/13

Answer [   ]

Q25. Which two fractions are equivalent?

A. 4/5 and 9/10

B. 10/20 and 20/20

C. 3/6 and 1/2

D. 1/2 and 5/11

Answer

Q26. Which two fractions are equivalent?

A. 5/6 and 20/23

B. 15/30 and 30/45

C. 12/30 and 6/10

D. 11/30 and 44/120

Answer

Q27. Which two fractions are equivalent?

A. 42/45 and 15/14

B. 52/64 and 13/16

C. 1/2 and 50/60

D. 3/4 and 30/50

Answer

Q28. Which two fractions are equivalent?

A. 5/3 and 3/5

B. 20/15 and 10/5

C. 3/4 and 60/80

D. 12/30 and 2/4

Answer

Q29. Which two fractions are equivalent?

A. 120/160 and 3/4

B. 130/150 and 13/14

C. 50/52 and 52/50

D. 3/4 and 1/2

Answer

Q30. Which two fractions are equivalent?

A. 25/50 and 20/30

B. 180/200 and 9/10

C. 4/5 and 5/4

D. 8/10 and 16/10

Answer

Q31. 3 1/2 - 1 1/4 =

A. 1 1/2

B. 3

C. 2 1/4

D. 1 3/4

Answer [   ]

Q32. 3 1/2 - 1 5/6 =

A. 1 3/6

B. 1 2/3

C. 1 1/4

D. 1 1/2

Answer [   ]

Q33. 5 3/5 – 2 1/4 =

A. 3 3/6

B. 4

C. 3 4/10

D. 3 7/20

Answer [   ]

Q34. 6 3/7 – 5 1/8 =

A. 1 17/56

B. 1 15/20

C. 1 15/40

D. 1 10/48

Answer

Q35. 7 3/5 − 5 2/3 =

A. 1 5/10

B. 1 14/15

C. 2

D. 1 13/15

Answer

Q36. Natalie ate 1 1/2 pizzas and Rachel ate 1 1/4. How much more pizza did Natalie eat than Rachel?

A. 1/2

B. 1/4

C. 2/5

D. 4/8

Answer

Q37. Sam ate 1 1/4 of cake and Robert ate 1 1/3 of the cake. How much more cake did Robert eat than Sam?

A. 2/3

B. 1/2

C. 1/12

D. 5/12

Answer [ ]

Q38. David ate 3 1/2 brownies. Elliott ate 5 3/4 of brownies. How much more brownies did Elliott eat than David?

A. 2 1/4

B. 2 1/2

C. 3

D. 1 3/4

Answer [ ]

Q39. Aarron ate 5 1/2 mini sausage rolls. Ryan ate 8 3/5 of mini sausage rolls. How much more mini sausage rolls did Ryan eat than Aarron?

A.3 1/2

B. 2 1/5

C. 3 3/10

D. 3 1/10

Answer [ ]

Q40. 4/3 ÷ 3/4 =

A. 1 9/7

B. 1 5/7

C. 1 7/9

D. 1 7/5

Answer

Q41. 6/4 ÷ 2/3 =

A. 2 1/2

B. 2 1/4

C. 2 3/4

D. 3

Answer

Q42. 4 ÷ 1/6 =

A. 30

B. 1/2

C. 24

D. 3/4

Answer

Q43. 6 ÷ 2/7 =

A. 21

B. 1/2

C. 21 1/2

D. 10/21

Answer

Q44. 8 ÷ 3/5 =

A. 31

B. 26

C. 13 1/3

D. 13 1/2

Answer

Q45. 4/5 x 3/4 =

A. 4/10

B. 1/4

C. 3/5

D. 2/3

Answer

Q46. 5/8 x 4/9 =

A. 3/18

B. 3/10

C. 4/12

D. 5/18

Answer

Q47. 10/3 x 11/4 =

A. 8 5/6

B. 11

C. 9 1/6

D. 10 1/6

Answer

Q48. What fraction is the shaded part?

A. 2 3/4

B. 2 1/4

C. 2 1/2

D. 2

Answer [ ]

Q49. What fraction is the shaded part?

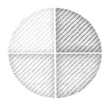 

A. 2

B. 1 3/4

C. 1 1/2

D. 1 1/4

Answer [ ]

Q50. What fraction is the shaded part?

A. 3 1/2

B. 3 1/4

C. 3 3/4

D. 3

Answer

Please now check your answers carefully before moving onto the next section of the guide.

ANSWERS TO IQ AND APTITUDE TEST SECTION 3

Q1. C

Q2. D

Q3. B

Q4. C

Q5. B

Q6. C

Q7. A

Q8. A

Q9. C

Q10. A

Q11. A

Q12. C

Q13. C

Q14. B

Q15. C

Q16. D

Q17. A

Q18. B

Q19. A

Q20. C

Q21. C

Q22. B

Q23. D

Q24. A

Q25. C

Q26. D

Q27. B

Q28. C

Q29. A

Q30. B

Q31. C

Q32. B

Q33. D

Q34. A

Q35. B

Q36. B

Q37. C

Q38. A

Q39. D

Q40. C

Q41. B

Q42. C

Q43. A

Q44. C

Q45. C

Q46. D

Q47. C

Q48. C

Q49. B

Q50. B

Now move onto the next section of the guide.

IQ & APTITUDE TEST
SECTION 4
(Ratios)

In IQ & Aptitude Test section 4 there are 30 questions and you have just 15 minutes to answer them

IQ AND APTITUDE TEST SECTION 4

Q1. Sam has 80p. Robert has £1.20.

What is the ratio of Sam's money to Robert's money, in its simplest form?

Answer

Q2. Elliott has £1.50. David has £2.20.

What is the ratio of Elliott's money to David's money, in its simplest form?

Answer

Q3. Mia has £4.50. Ellie has £6.50.

What is the ratio of Mia's money to Ellie's money, in its simplest form?

Answer

Q4. Liz has £12.00. Steph has £8.50.

What is the ratio of Liz's money to Steph's money, in its simplest form?

Answer

Q5. Ryan has £11.20. Harrison has £9.10.

What is the ratio of Ryan's money to Harrison's money, in its simplest form?

Answer

Q6. Martin has 90p. Sam has £1.80.

What is the ratio of Martin's money to Sam's money, in its simplest form?

Answer

Q7. Rachel has 340p. Tina has 480p.

What is the ratio of Rachel's money to Tina's money, in its simplest form?

Answer

Q8. Peter has £15.20. Jim has £20.80

What is the ratio of Peter's money to Jim's money, in its simplest form?

Answer

Q9. Gemma has 580p. Sandra has £2.40.

What is the ratio of Gemma's money to Sandra's money, in its simplest form?

Answer

Q10. Billy has 560p. Robert has £16.80.

What is the ratio of Billy's money to Robert's money, in its simplest form?

Answer

Q11. A newspaper includes 16 pages of sport and 8 pages of TV. What is the ratio of sport to TV? Give your answer in its simplest form.

Answer

Q12. A magazine includes 24 pages of fashion and 8 pages of lifestyle. What is the ratio of fashion to lifestyle? Give your answer in its simplest form.

Answer

Q13. A newsletter includes 12 pages on current affairs and 3 pages on healthcare. What is the ratio of current affairs to healthcare? Give your answer in its simplest form.

Answer

Q14. A book contains 240 pages for its novel and 24 pages for introductions and summaries. What is the ratio of novel pages to introductions and summaries? Give your answer in its simplest form.

Answer

Q15. A newspaper has 15 pages of current affairs, 12 pages of lifestyle and 18 pages for sport. What is the ratio to current affairs to lifestyle to sport? Give your answer in its simplest form.

Answer

Q16. A magazine includes 36 pages of lifestyle and 12 pages of self-help. What is the ratio of lifestyle to self-help? Give your answer in its simplest form.

Answer [   ]

Q17. A newspaper has 40 pages of news articles and 18 pages of advertisements. What is the ratio of news articles to advertisements? Give your answer in its simplest form.

Answer [   ]

Q18. A school has to mark 180 English papers and 170 Maths papers. What is the ratio of English papers to Maths papers? Give your answer in its simplest form.

Answer [   ]

Q19. A teacher has to mark 36 English Literature tests and 24 English Language tests. What is the ratio of Literature to Language tests? Give your answer in its simplest form.

Answer [   ]

Q20. A newspaper includes 38 pages of world events and 18 pages of sports. What is the ratio of world events to sports? Give your answer in its simplest form.

Answer [   ]

Q21. There are 18 girls and 12 boys in a class. What is the ratio of girls to boys? Give your answer in its simplest form.

Answer [   ]

Q22. There are 16 girls and 4 boys in a school choir. What is the ratio of girls to boys? Give your answer in its simplest form.

Answer [   ]

Q23. There are 24 girls and 32 boys in a P.E lesson. What is the ratio of girls to boys? Give your answer in its simplest form.

Answer [   ]

Q24. There are 60 girls and 65 boys in the lunch hall at school. What is the ratio of girls to boys? Give your answer in its simplest form.

Answer [   ]

Q25. There are 25 female teachers and 5 male teachers at a secondary school. What is the ratio of female to male teachers? Give your answer in its simplest form.

Answer [   ]

Q26. There are 22 girls and 14 boys in a class. What is the ratio of girls to boys? Give your answer in its simplest form.

Answer [   ]

Q27. There are 40 parents and 92 children taking part in sports day. What is the ratio of parents to children? Give your answer in its simplest form.

Answer [   ]

Q28. There are 36 female teachers and 8 male teachers at a secondary school. What is the ratio of female to male teachers? Give your answer in its simplest form.

Answer [   ]

Q29. There are 22 girls and 28 boys taking part in a talent contest. What is the ratio of girls to boys? Give your answer in its simplest form.

Answer [   ]

Q30. There are 14 girls and 20 boys in a class. What is the ratio of girls to boys? Give your answer in its simplest form.

Answer [   ]

Now check your answers before moving onto the next section of the guide.

ANSWERS TO IQ AND APTITUDE TEST SECTION 4

Q1. 2:3

EXPLANATION: One amount is in pence, the other in pounds. We have to convert Robert's amount into pence first. £1.20 = 120p. Now the ratio is 80:120. Both sides are divisible by 40. Dividing both sides by 40 gives 2:3. So the ratio is 2:3.

Q2. 15:22

EXPLANATION: Both amounts are in pounds. We have to convert both amounts into pence. £1.50 = 150p. £2.20 = 220p. Now the ratio is 150:220. Both sides are divisible by 10. Dividing both sides by 10 gives 15:22. So the ratio is 15:22.

Q3. 9:13

EXPLANATION: Both amounts are in pounds. We have to convert both amounts into pence. £4.50 = 450p. £6.50 = 650p. Now the ratio is 450:650. Both sides are divisible by 50. Dividing both sides by 50 gives 9:13. So the ratio is 9:13.

Q4. 24:17

EXPLANATION: Both amounts are in pounds. We have to convert both amounts into pence. £12.00 = 1200p. £8.50 = 850p. Now the ratio is 1200:850. Both sides are divisible by 50. Dividing both sides by 50 gives 24:17. So the ratio is 24:17.

Q5. 16:13

EXPLANATION: Both amounts are in pounds. We have to convert both amounts into pence. £11.20 = 1120p. £9.10 = 910p. Now the ratio is 1120:910. Both sides are divisible by 70. Dividing both sides by 70 gives 16:13. So the ratio is 16:13.

Q6. 1:2

EXPLANATION: One amount is in pence, the other in pounds. We have to convert Sam's amount into pence first. £1.80 = 180p. Now the ratio is 90:180. Both sides are divisible by 90. Dividing both sides by 90 gives 1:2. So the ratio is 1:2.

Q7. 17:24

EXPLANATION: Both amounts are in pence. The ratio is 340:480. Both sides are divisible by 20. Dividing both sides by 20 gives 17:24. So the ratio is 17:24.

Q8. 19:26

EXPLANATION: Both amounts are in pounds. We have to convert both amounts into pence. £15.20 = 1520p. £20.80 = 2080p. Now the ratio is 1520:2080. Both sides are divisible by 80. Dividing both sides by 80 gives 19:26. So the ratio is 19:26.

Q9. 29:12

EXPLANATION: One amount is in pence, the other in pounds. We have to convert Sandra's amount into pence first. £2.40 = 240p. Now the ratio is 580:240. Both sides are divisible by 20. Dividing both sides by 20 gives 29:12. So the ratio is 29:12.

Q10. 1:3

EXPLANATION: One amount is in pence, the other in pounds. We have to convert Robert's amount into pence first. £16.80 = 1680p. Now the ratio is 560:1680. Both sides are divisible by 560. Dividing both sides by 560 gives 1:3. So the ratio is 1:3.

Q11. 2:1

EXPLANATION: The answer is 2:1. You can divide both sides of 16:8 by 8.

Q12. 3:1

EXPLANATION: The answer is 3:1. You can divide both sides of 24:8 by 8.

Q13. 4:1

EXPLANATION: The answer is 4:1. You can divide both sides of 12:3 by 3.

Q14. 10:1

EXPLANATION: The answer is 10:1. You can divide both sides of 240:24 by 24.

Q15. 5:4:6

EXPLANATION: The answer is 5:4:6. You can divide 15:12:18 by 3.

Q16. 3:1

EXPLANATION: The answer is 3:1. You can divide both sides of 36:12 by 12.

Q17. 20:9

EXPLANATION: The answer is 20:9. You can divide both sides of 40:18 by 2.

Q18. 18:17

EXPLANATION: The answer is 18:17. You can divide both sides of 180:170 by 10.

Q19. 3:2

EXPLANATION: The answer is 3:2. You can divide both sides of 36:24 by 12.

Q20. 19:9

EXPLANATION: The answer is 19:9. You can divide both sides of 38:18 by 2.

Q21. 3:2

EXPLANATION: The ratio of girls to boys is 18:12. However, both sides of this ratio are divisible by 6. Dividing by 6 gives 3:2. 3 has no common factors (apart from 1). So the simplest form of the ratio is 3:2. This means there are 3 girls in the class for every 2 boys.

Q22. 4:1

EXPLANATION: The ratio of girls to boys is 16:4. However, both sides of this ratio are divisible by 4. Dividing by 4 gives 4:1. So the simplest form of the ratio is 4:1. This means there are 4 girls in the choir for every 1 boy.

Q23. 3:4

EXPLANATION: The ratio of girls to boys is 24:32. However, both sides of this ratio are divisible by 8. Dividing by 8 gives 3:4. 3 has no common factors (apart from 1). So the simplest form of the ratio is 3:4. This means there are 3 girls in the class for every 4 boys.

Q24. 12:13

EXPLANATION: The ratio of girls to boys is 60:65. However, both sides of this ratio are divisible by 5. Dividing by 5 gives 12:13. 13 has no common factors (apart from 1). So the simplest form of the ratio is 12:13. This means there are 12 girls in the lunch hall for every 13 boys.

Q25. 5:1

EXPLANATION: The ratio of female to male teachers is 25:5. However, both sides of this ratio are divisible by 5. Dividing by 5 gives 5:1. 5 has no common factors (apart

from 1). So the simplest form of the ratio is 5:1. This means there are 5 female teachers for every 5 male teachers.

Q26. 11:7

EXPLANATION: The ratio of girls to boys is 22:14. However, both sides of this ratio are divisible by 2. Dividing by 2 gives 11:7. 7 and 11 have no common factors (apart from 1). So the simplest form of the ratio is 11:7. This means there are 11 girls in the class for every 7 boys.

Q27. 10:23

EXPLANATION: The ratio of parents to children is 40:92. However, both sides of this ratio are divisible by 4. Dividing by 4 gives 10:23. 23 has no common factors (apart from 1). So the simplest form of the ratio is 10:23. This means there are 10 parents for every 23 children.

Q28. 9:2

EXPLANATION: The ratio of female to male teachers is 36:8. However, both sides of this ratio are divisible by 4. Dividing by 4 gives 9:2. So the simplest form of the ratio is 9:2. This means there are 9 female teachers for every 2 male teachers.

Q29. 11:14

EXPLANATION: The ratio of girls to boys is 22:28. However, both sides of this ratio are divisible by 2. Dividing by 2 gives 11:14. 11 has no common factors (apart from 1). So the simplest form of the ratio is 11:14. This means there are 11 girls in the talent contest for every 14 boys.

Q30. 7:10

EXPLANATION: The ratio of girls to boys is 14:20. However, both sides of this ratio are divisible by 2. Dividing by 2 gives 7:10. 7 has no common factors (apart from 1).

So the simplest form of the ratio is 7:10. This means there are 7 girls in the class for every 10 boys.

Now move onto the next section of the guide.

IQ & APTITUDE TEST
SECTION 5
(Number sequence)

In IQ & Aptitude Test section 5 there are 30 questions and you have just 15 minutes to answer them

IQ AND APTITUDE TEST SECTION 5

Q1. Look carefully for the pattern, and then choose which pair of numbers comes next.

5 7 9 11 13 15 17

A. 18, 19

B. 19, 21

C. 19, 20

D. 21, 23

Answer

Q2. Look carefully for the pattern, and then choose which pair of numbers comes next.

3 5 21 8 10 21 13 15

A. 18, 20

B. 18, 21

C. 21, 18

D. 17, 21

E. 17, 20

Answer

Q3. Look carefully for the pattern, and then choose which pair of numbers comes next.

1   3   6   10   15   21   28

A. 36, 45

B. 35, 45

C. 30, 36

D. 36, 42

E. 35, 46

Answer

Q4. Look carefully for the pattern, and then choose which pair of numbers comes next.

2   4   55   8   16   55   32

A. 64, 128

B. 55, 64

C. 55, 110

D. 64, 55

E. None of the above

Answer

Q5. Look carefully for the pattern, and then choose which pair of numbers comes next.

1   4   9   16   25   36   49

A. 54, 63

B. 63, 74

C. 51, 80

D. 56, 82

E. 64, 81

Answer

Q6. Look carefully for the pattern, and then choose which pair of numbers comes next.

0 1 1 2 3 5 8

A. 12, 18

B. 13, 21

C. 15, 23

D. 13, 22

E. 15, 25

Answer

Q7. Look carefully for the pattern, and then choose which pair of numbers comes next.

27   25   87   23   21   87   19

A. 16, 13

B. 17, 15

C. 16, 87

D. 17, 87

E 87, 17

Answer

Q8. Look carefully for the pattern, and then choose which pair of numbers comes next.

1   3   7   15   31   63   127

A. 220, 440

B. 255, 511

C. 136, 210

D. 187, 316

E. 254, 508

Answer

Q9. Look carefully for the pattern, and then choose which pair of numbers comes next.

1   3   6   10   15   21   28

A. 42, 56

B. 42, 48

C. 30, 36

D. 32, 36

E. 36, 45

Answer [   ]

Q10. Look carefully for the pattern, and then choose which pair of numbers comes next.

1   8   27   90   64   125   216

A. 90, 343

B. 343, 512

C. 343, 90

D. 90, 512

E. 380, 418

Answer [   ]

Q11. Look carefully for the pattern, and then choose which pair of numbers comes next.

8   13   18   23   28   33   38

A. 42, 48

B. 42, 47

C. 43, 48

D. 45, 48

Answer [   ]

Q12. Look carefully for the pattern, and then choose which pair of numbers comes next.

4   8   80   12   16   80   20   24

A. 80, 28

B. 28, 32

C. 32, 80

D. 28, 80

E. 28, 30

Answer [   ]

Q13. Look carefully for the pattern, and then choose which pair of numbers comes next.

3   5   8   12   17   23   30

A. 36, 45

B. 38, 48

C. 32, 40

D. 38, 47

E. 35, 42

Answer [   ]

Q14. Look carefully for the pattern, and then choose which pair of numbers comes next.

6   12   24   60   48   96   192

A. 384, 748

B. 362, 60

C. 65, 360

D. 60, 381

E. None of the above

Answer [   ]

Q15. Look carefully for the pattern, and then choose which pair of numbers comes next.

16   25   36   49   64   81   100

A. 120, 144

B. 121, 144

C. 121, 146

D. 120, 184

E. None of the above

Answer [   ]

Q16. Look carefully for the pattern, and then choose which pair of numbers comes next.

0   8   8   16   24   40   64

A. 121, 182

B. 120, 180

C. 100, 136

D. 104, 132

E. 104, 168

Answer [   ]

Q17. Q7. Look carefully for the pattern, and then choose which pair of numbers comes next.

42   36   50   30   24   50   18

A. 12, 50

B. 50, 12

C. 16, 12

D. 16, 14

E. None of the above

Answer [   ]

Q18. Look carefully for the pattern, and then choose which pair of numbers comes next.

9   21   45   93   189   381   765

A. 1480, 3890

B. 1522, 3080

C. 1533, 3069

D. 1458, 3076

E. None of the above

Answer

Q19. Look carefully for the pattern, and then choose which pair of numbers comes next.

1   3   9   27   81   243   729

A. 2178, 6791

B. 2187, 6561

C. 1533, 3096

D. 1353, 3906

E. 1335, 3609

Answer

Q20. Look carefully for the pattern, and then choose which pair of numbers comes next.

27   64   125   101   216   343   512

A. 101, 729

B. 729, 1000

C. 729, 101

D. 101, 1000

E. None of the above

Answer

Q21. Look carefully for the pattern, and then choose which pair of numbers comes next.

5   8   14   26   50   98   194

A. 296, 412

B. 296, 408

C. 384, 760

D. 386, 770

E. 386, 612

Answer

Q22. Look carefully for the pattern, and then choose which pair of numbers comes next.

84   80   60   76   72   60   68

A. 62, 60

B. 60, 64

C. 64, 60

D. 60, 62

E. None of the above

Answer

Q23. Look carefully for the pattern, and then choose which pair of numbers comes next.

1   5   25   125   625   3125

A. 15,625, 78,125

B. 14,000, 16,250

C. 15,125, 75,125

D. 20,205, 80,250

E. None of the above

Answer

Q24. Look carefully for the pattern, and then choose which pair of numbers comes next.

1   8   22   50   106   218   442

A. 890, 1768

B. 990, 1786

C. 890, 1786

D. 980, 1786

E. 980, 1768

Answer

Q25. Look carefully for the pattern, and then choose which pair of numbers comes next.

3   5   11   29   83   245

A. 317, 1298

B. 317, 1289

C. 731, 2198

D. 713, 2198

E. 731, 2189

Answer [   ]

Q26. Look carefully for the pattern, and then choose which pair of numbers comes next.

0   7   7   14   21   35   56

A. 91, 147

B. 90, 146

C. 65, 125

D. 65, 121

E. 65, 136

Answer [   ]

Q27. Look carefully for the pattern, and then choose which pair of numbers comes next.

9   18   27   36   45   54   63

A. 73, 82

B. 72, 80

C. 81, 90

D. 72, 81

E. None of the above

Answer

Q28. Look carefully for the pattern, and then choose which pair of numbers comes next.

62   57   80   52   47   80   42

A. 80, 36

B. 36, 80

C. 80, 37

D. 80, 38

E. 37, 80

Answer

Q29. Look carefully for the pattern, and then choose which pair of numbers comes next.

9   12   60   14   17   60   19

A. 24, 60

B. 60, 22

C. 22, 60

D. 60, 24

E. 60, 21

Answer [   ]

Q30. Look carefully for the pattern, and then choose which pair of numbers comes next.

13   17   50   20   24   50   27

A. 30, 50

B. 50, 31

C. 50, 32

D. 32, 50

E. 31, 50

Answer [   ]

Now check your answers carefully before moving onto the next section of the guide.

ANSWERS TO IQ AND APTITUDE TEST SECTION 5

Q1. B

Explanation: This is a series of repetition. The regular series adds 2 to every number.

Q2. C

Explanation: This is an alternating addition series with repetition, in which a random number, 21, is interpolated as every third number. The regular series adds 2, then 3, then 2, and so on, with 21 repeated after each "add 2" step.

Q3. A

Explanation: This is an alternating addition series. The regular series adds 2, then 3, then 4, then 5 (increasing by 1 every time) and so on.

Q4. D

Explanation: This is a series of repetition, in which a random number, 55, is interpolated as every third number. The regular series is multiplied by 2 each time. (The number doubles as the sequence progresses, with 55 repeated as every third number).

Q5. E

Explanation: The regular series are the square numbers to whole numbers. The sequence starts from (1 x 1), (2 x 2), (3 x 3), (4 x 4) and so on.

Q6. B

Explanation: This is a Fibonacci number sequence. The sequence follows the pattern of adding the two numbers before it together. For example, the 8 is found by adding the 5 and the 3 together.

Q7. D

Explanation: This is an alternating addition series with repetition, in which a random number, 87, is interpolated as every third number. The regular series subtracts 2 each time.

Q8. B

Explanation: This sequence follows the pattern of doubling the number and adding 1. For example, to get 15, 7 was doubled to give 14 plus 1 = 15.

Q9. E

Explanation: This is a triangular number sequence. It uses the pattern of the number of dots which forms a triangle. By adding another row of dots (which increases by 1 each time) and counting all the dots, we can find the next number of the sequence.

Q10. A

Explanation: This is a cube numbered sequence, with an alternating addition series, in which a random number, 90, is interpolated as every fourth number. The regular sequence follows the pattern of (1 x 1 x 1), (2 x 2 x 2), (3 x 3 x 3), (4 x 4 x 4) and so on.

Q11. C

Explanation: This is a series of repetition. The regular series adds 5 to every number.

Q12. A

Explanation: This is an alternating addition series with repetition, in which a random number, 80, is interpolated as every third number. The regular series adds 4 each time, with 80 being interpolated as every third number.

Q13. D

Explanation: This is an alternating addition series. The regular series adds 2, then 3, then 4, then 5 (increasing by 1 every time) and so on.

Q14. E

Explanation: This is a series of repetition, in which a random number, 60, is interpolated as every fourth number. The regular series is multiplied by 2 each time. (The number doubles as the sequence progresses, with 60 repeated as every fourth number). So, the next two numbers would be 60 and 384.

Q15. B

Explanation: The regular series are the square numbers to whole numbers. The sequence starts from (4 x 4), (5 x 5), (6 x 6), (7 x 7) and so on.

Q16. E

Explanation: This is a Fibonacci number sequence. The sequence follows the pattern of adding the two numbers before it together. For example, the 16 is found by adding the 8 and the 8 together.

Q17. A

Explanation: This is an alternating addition series with repetition, in which a random number, 50, is interpolated as every third number. The regular series subtracts 6 each time.

Q18. C

Explanation: This sequence follows the pattern of doubling the number and adding 3. For example, to get 21, 9 was doubled to give 18 plus 3 = 21.

Q19. B

Explanation: This sequence follows the pattern of multiplying the previous number by 3 to give you the next number in the sequence.

Q20. A

Explanation: This is a cube numbered sequence, with an alternating addition series, in which a random number, 101, is interpolated as every fourth number. The regular sequence follows the pattern of (3 x 3 x 3), (4 x 4 x 4), (5 x 5 x 5), (6 x 6 x 6) and so on.

Q21. D

Explanation: The sequence follows the pattern of doubling the previous number and subtracting 2. For example 8 x 2 = 16 – 2 = 14 and so on.

Q22. C

Explanation: This is a series of repetition, in which a random number, 60, is interpolated as every third number. The regular series subtracts 4 each time, with 60 being interpolated as every third number.

Q23. A

Explanation: The sequence follows the pattern of multiplying the previous number by 5 to give you the next number in the sequence.

Q24. C

Explanation: The sequence follows the pattern of adding 3 and then multiplying it by 2. For example, the next number after 8 in the sequence would be 22 (8 + 3 = 11 x 2 = 22).

Q25. E

Explanation: The sequence follows the pattern of multiplying by 3, then subtracting 4. For example, the next number after 11 would be 29 (11 x 3 = 33 – 4 = 29).

Q26. A

Explanation: This is a Fibonacci number sequence. The sequence follows the pattern of adding the two numbers before it together. For example, the 21 is found by adding the 14 and the 7 together.

Q27. D

Explanation: The sequence follows the pattern of multiplying the number by 9 to give you the next number in the sequence.

Q28. E

Explanation: This is a series of repetition, in which a random number, 80, is interpolated as every third number. The regular subtracts 5 each time, with 80 being repeated for every third number.

Q29. C

Explanation: This is an alternating addition series with repetition, in which a random number, 60, is interpolated as every third number. The regular series adds 3, then 2, then 3, and so on, with 60 repeated after each "add 3" step.

Q30. E

Explanation: This is an alternating addition series with repetition, in which a random number, 50, is interpolated as every third number. The regular series adds 4, then 3, then 4, and so on, with 50 repeated after each "add 4" step.

Now move onto the next section of the guide.

IQ & APTITUDE TEST
SECTION 6
(Spatial aptitude)

In IQ & Aptitude Test section 6 there are 3 parts, each consisting of 5 questions. You have just 5 minutes to answer each part.

IQ AND APTITUDE TEST SECTION 6 (PART 1)

You have just 5 minutes to answer part 1.

Q1. Which is the missing section?

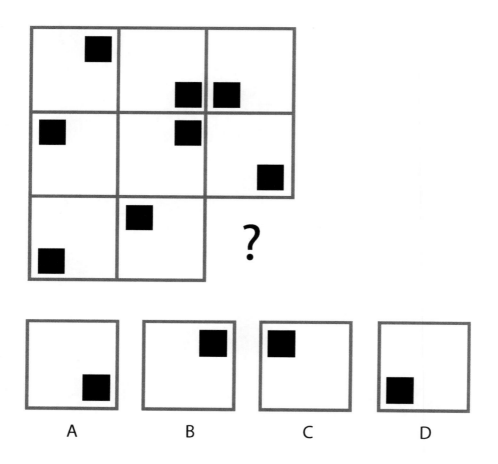

Q2. Which is the missing section?

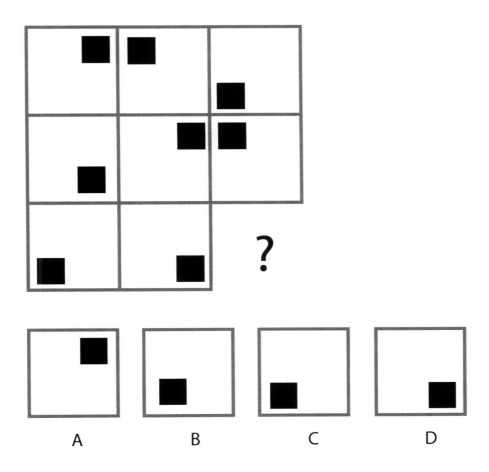

A   B   C   D

Answer

Q3. Which is the missing section?

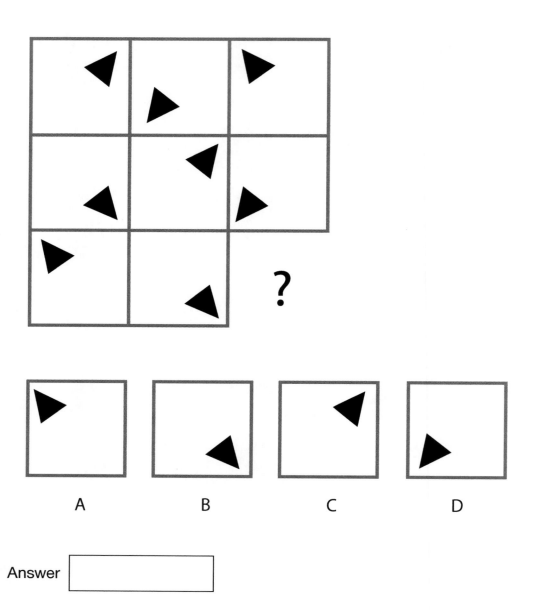

A   B   C   D

Answer

Q4. Which is the missing section?

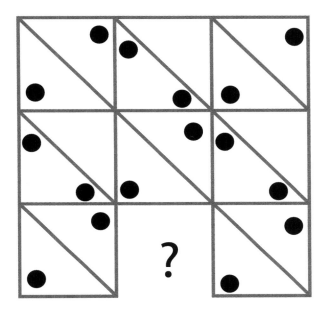

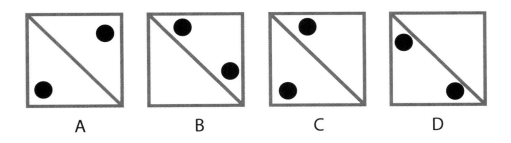

Answer [   ]

Q5. Which is the missing section?

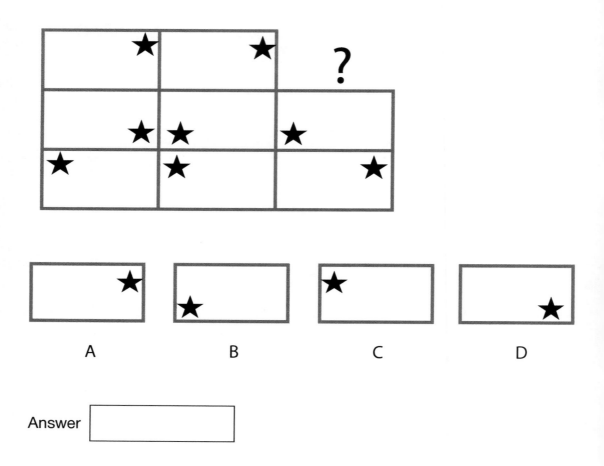

Answer [ ]

Now please check your answers carefully before moving onto part 2.

ANSWERS TO IQ AND APTITUDE TEST SECTION 6 (PART 1)

Q1. B

Moving from left to right in each row, the black square rotates around each square in a clockwise manner.

Q2. A

Moving from left to right in each row, the black square rotates around each square in an anti- clockwise manner.

Q3. C

Moving from left to right in each row, the black triangle follows the sequence top right, bottom left, top left, bottom right.

Q4. D

Moving from left to right in each row, the two black dots follows the sequence of square 1 containing a black dot in the top right corner and the bottom left corner. The second box has the dots in the first half of the square, in the top and bottom position.

Q5. D

Moving from left to right in each row, the star stays in the same position for two boxes. It then rotates around each rectangle in a clockwise motion, stays the same for two boxes and continues this pattern.

Now move onto part 2.

IQ AND APTITUDE TEST SECTION 6 (PART 2)

You have just 5 minutes to answer part 2.

Q1. Which figure is identical to the first?

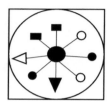 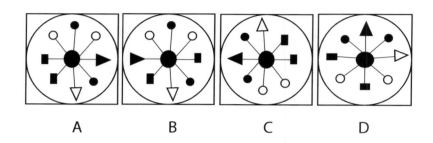

Answer [   ]

Q2. Which figure is identical to the first?

 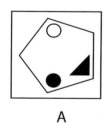   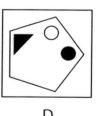

Answer [   ]

Q3. Which figure is identical to the first?

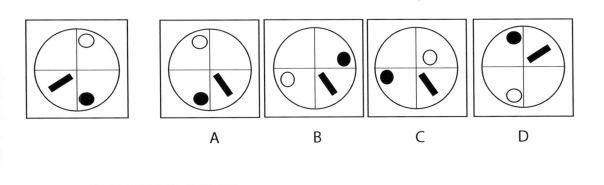

Answer

Q4. Which figure is identical to the first?

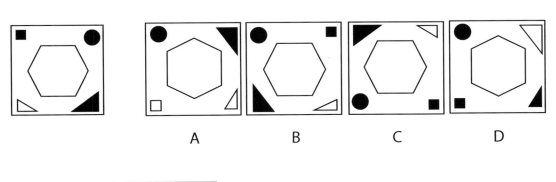

Answer

Q5. Which figure is identical to the first?

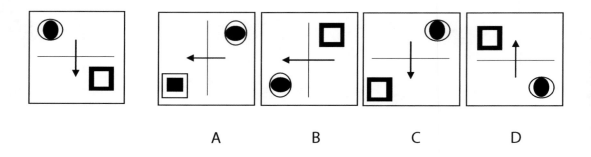

A B C D

Answer

ANSWERS TO IQ AND APTITUDE TEST SECTION 6 (PART 2)

Q1. A

Only one of the figures is an exact rotation of the first – the others are reflections or slightly modified in some way.

Q2. B

Only one of the figures is an exact rotation of the first – the others are reflections or slightly modified in some way.

Q3. D

Only one of the figures is an exact rotation of the first – the others are reflections or slightly modified in some way.

Q4. C

Only one of the figures is an exact rotation of the first – the others are reflections or slightly modified in some way.

Q5. D

Only one of the figures is an exact rotation of the first – the others are reflections or slightly modified in some way.

Now move onto part 3.

IQ AND APTITUDE TEST SECTION 6 (PART 3)

You have just 5 minutes to answer part 3.

Q1. Which group of shapes can be assembled to make the shape shown?

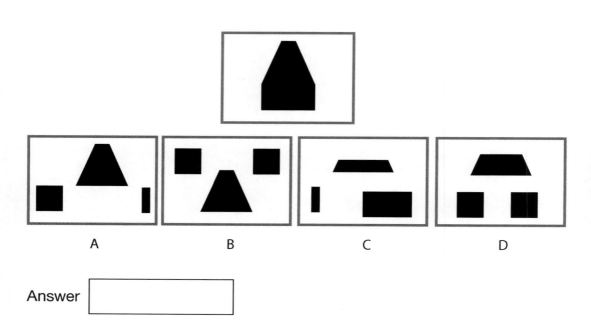

A   B   C   D

Answer

Q2. Which group of shapes can be assembled to make the shape shown?

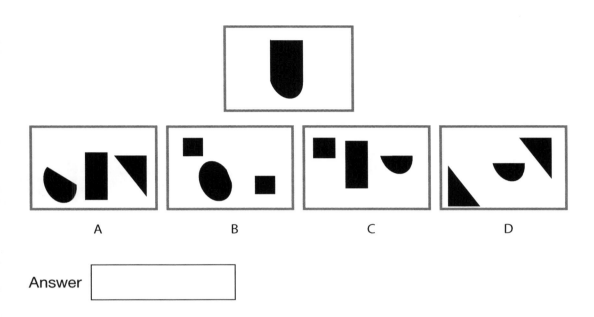

Answer

Q3. Which group of shapes can be assembled to make the shape shown?

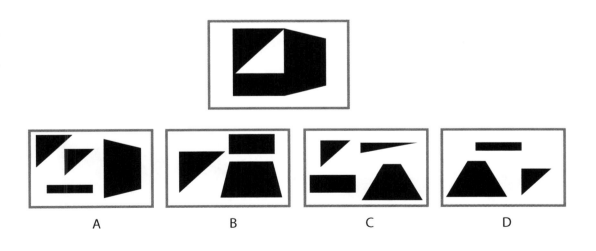

Answer

Q4. Which group of shapes can be assembled to make the shape shown?

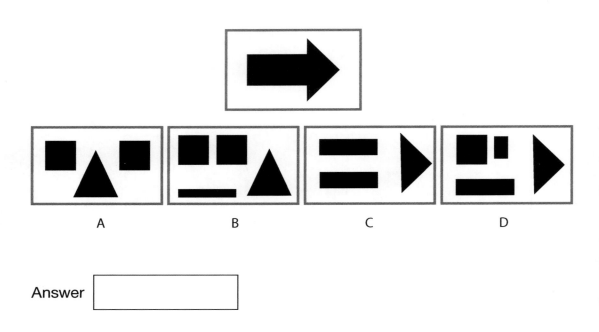

A   B   C   D

Answer

Q5. Which group of shapes can be assembled to make the shape shown?

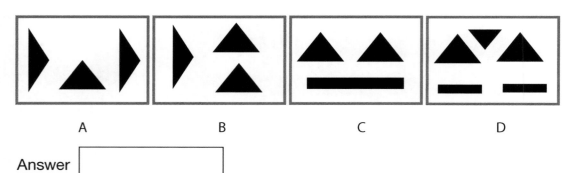

A   B   C   D

Answer

ANSWERS TO IQ AND APTITUDE TEST SECTION 6 (PART 3)

Q1. B

Q2. D

Q3. B

Q4. C

Q5. A

Now move onto the next section of the guide.

IQ & APTITUDE TEST
SECTION 7
(Grammar and Comprehension)

*In IQ & Aptitude Test section 7 there are 5 parts.
The time limit for each part is indicated
at the beginning of the test.*

IQ AND APTITUDE TEST SECTION 7 (PART 1)

You have 10 minutes to complete part 1.

Q1.

Firefighters are people whose _____ job it is to put out fires. However, what most people don't realise is that nowadays, firefighters have a number of roles. They are often called to car _____ when people need to be cut out of their cars, they are called to _____ buildings, search and rescues, stuck elevators etc. The firefighter service _____ a rescue service, it is not just a fire service.

Insert the 4 words below into their correct positions within the text.

collisions

provides

collapsed

primary

Q2.

There are many types of roles within the police force. Some have been trained for special duties such as counter _____, surveillance, child protection and investigating _____ into major crimes. Police hold a high level of responsibility. Their aim is to provide a _____ that protects the people and places of communities. They enforce law _____ and guidelines for society to uphold; and punish those who do not conform to the social norms of society.

Insert the 4 words below into their correct positions within the text.

techniques

service

procedures

terrorism

Q3.

Paramedics are healthcare _____ that deal with accidents and medical emergencies. A paramedic is one of the first healthcare professionals to attend the scene of _____ or emergency. They will assess the patient's condition and treat them accordingly. They can _____ oxygen, drugs and use high-end technical _____ such as defibrillators and spinal splints if necessary.

Insert the 4 words below into their correct positions within the text.

administer

equipment

professionals

accident

Q4.

Law is the system of rules, guidelines and conducts established by the _____ government that maintains a safe and stable society. A lawyer is a person that is learned in law; whether that be as an _____, counsel, or solicitor. They deal with _____ theories and knowledge and apply it to individualised _____. No two cases are the same, and so they have to be treated very differently.

Insert the 4 words below into their correct positions within the text.

attorney

sovereign

circumstances

legal

Q5.

Journalism is a _____ style and inquiry based method that provides a service to the public with _____, data and information regarding newsworthy events. Journalistic _____ can vary from print publishing to electronic publishing, television, web and even mobile phone apps. Journalism is based on the principles of truth, _____ independence and integrity that forms different types of expressions and communications.

Insert the 4 words below into their correct positions within the text.

news

mediums

editorial

literary

Q6.

Many people do not experience the world of _____. Travelling offers so much insight, knowledge and experience of the world, that it allows people to see the world from a whole new _____. Experiencing the natural _____ and historical landmarks provides not only a _____ experience but knowledge and understanding about the world we live in.

Insert the 4 words below into their correct positions within the text.

perspective

beauty

memorable

travel

Q7.

The job role of farming is more strenuous than people think. Farmers are _____ in the world of agriculture. Most farmers wake up at dawn to begin their day of duties. Duties such as cropping, _____, planting, and feeding are a few typical duties of farmers. Farmers work long hours and are constantly _____ and on-going. Not everybody would be cut out for the role of farming due to its long hours, _____ work and constant care to its products and/or livestock.

Insert the 4 words below into their correct positions within the text.

harvesting

active

strenuous

engaged

Q8.

It is a difficult time for students to come straight out of university and into a job. _____ being educated at degree level, they are yet to have a great deal of _____ in the chosen area of their choice. Students are _____ to gain as much experience where possible regarding their career, in hope that they can leave university with a good degree grade and experience, and will put them one _____ closer to achieving their goals.

Insert the 4 words below into their correct positions within the text.

advised

experience

step

despite

Q9.

Most parents want an _____ and healthy lifestyle for their children. Many schools offer clubs for children to join. Clubs such as football, gymnastics, dance and boxing are offered in _____ in order to keep children active. Healthy living and active _____ has recently been debated in the news and it is _____ that children are not being as active or as healthy as they should be.

Insert the 4 words below into their correct positions within the text.

schools

lifestyles

believed

active

Q10.

Most parents agreed that bedtime reading with their children is the only time they get to spend some _____ time together. Many parents spend a lot of their time working in order to keep a roof over their families head; and so it is difficult for them to spend time as a _____. However, not all parents have bedtime reading with their children; and is _____ that spending this quality of time with their children _____ their parenting skills and betters their family lifestyle.

Insert the 4 words below into their correct positions within the text.

family

believed

enhances

quality

Now check your answers before moving onto part 2.

ANSWERS TO IQ AND APTITUDE TEST SECTION 7 (PART 1)

Q1.

Firefighters are people whose primary job it is to put out fires. However, what most people don't realise is that nowadays, firefighters have a number of roles. They are often called to car collisions when people need to be cut out of their cars, they are called to collapsed buildings, search and rescues, stuck elevators etc. The firefighter service provides a rescue service, it is not just a fire service.

Q2.

There are many types of roles within the police force. Some have been trained for special duties such as counter-terrorism, surveillance, child protection and investigating techniques into major crimes. Police hold a high level of responsibility. Their aim is to provide a service that protects the people and places of communities. They enforce law procedures and guidelines for society to uphold; and punish those who do not conform to the social norms of society.

Q3.

Paramedics are healthcare professionals that deal with accidents and medical emergencies. A paramedic is one of the first healthcare professionals to attend the scene of accident or emergency. They will assess the patient's condition and treat them accordingly. They can administer oxygen, drugs and use high-end technical equipment such as defibrillators and spinal splints if necessary.

Q4.

Law is the system of rules, guidelines and conducts established by the sovereign government that maintains a safe and stable society. A lawyer is a person that is learned in law; whether that be as an attorney, counsel or solicitor. They deal with legal theories and knowledge and apply it to individualised circumstances. No two cases are the same, and so they have to be treated very differently.

Q5.

Journalism is a literary style and inquiry based method that provides a service to the public with news, data and information regarding newsworthy events. Journalistic mediums can vary from print publishing to electronic publishing, newspapers, television, web and even mobile phones. It is based on the principles of truth, editorial independence and integrity that forms different types of expressions and communications.

Q6.

Many people do not experience the world of travel. Travelling offers so much insight, knowledge and experience of the world, that it allows people to see the world from a whole new perspective. Experiencing the natural beauty and historical landmarks provides not only a memorable experience but knowledge and understanding about the world we live in.

Q7.

The job role of farming is more strenuous than people think. Farmers are engaged in the world of agriculture. Most farmers wake up at dawn to begin their day of duties. Duties such as cropping, harvesting, planting, and feeding are a few typical duties of farmers. Farmers work long hours and are constantly active and on-going. Not everybody would be cut out for the role of farming due to its long hours, strenuous work and constant care to its products and/or livestock.

Q8.

It is a difficult time for students to come straight out of university and into a job. Despite being educated at degree level, they are yet to have a great deal of experience in the chosen area of their choice. Students are advised to gain as much experience where possible regarding their career, in hope that they can leave university with a good degree grade and experience, and will put them one step closer to achieving their goals.

Q9.

Most parents want an active and healthy lifestyle for their children. Many schools offer clubs for children to join. Clubs such as football, gymnastics, dance and boxing are offered in schools in order to keep children active. Healthy living and active lifestyles has recently been debated in the news and it is believed that children are not being as active or as healthy as they should be.

Q10.

Most parents agreed that bedtime reading with their children is the only time they get to spend some quality time together. Many parents spend a lot of their time working in order to keep a roof over their families head; and so it is difficult for them to spend time as a family. However, not all parents have bedtime reading with their children; and is believed that spending this quality of time with their children enhances their parenting skills and betters their family lifestyle.

Now move onto part 2.

IQ AND APTITUDE TEST SECTION 7 (PART 2)

You have 10 minutes to complete part 2.

Q1. The pilot _____ the helicopter back to basecamp due _____ the strong winds and _____ down pour.

Which of the following combinations of words is the only one which can be inserted into the sentence?

A. navigates, to, terrential

B. navegates, to, terrential

C. navigator, two, torrential

D. navigated, to, torrential

E. navigated, to, terrential

Answer

Q2. Prior to the airplane taking off, the _____ informs _____ about the safety _____ and key information about flying.

Which of the following combinations of words is the only one which can be inserted into the sentence?

A. stewardess, passengers, procedures

B. steward's, passangers, procedure

C. stewardess, passenger, procedure

D. stewardess, passenger, proseedure

E. Stewardest, passengors, procedure

Answer

Q3. The police _____ holding a suspect on very little _____. If they do not find any other proof, they will have to let the suspect go based on law _____.

Which one the following combinations of words is the only one which can be inserted into the sentence?

A. where, evidence, enforcements

B. were, evidance, inforcements

C. were, evidence, enforcements

D. wear, evidonce, enforcement

E. were, evidence, inforcement

Answer

Q4. The police followed through on a _____ given by someone who _____ a drunk man becoming aggressive at a store owner. They decided to send out a patrol car to _____ and deal with the situation.

Which one the following combinations of words is the only one which can be inserted into the sentence?

A. statement, witnesses, analyze

B. statement, witness, analise

C. statment, witnessed, analyse

D. statement, witnessed, analyse

E. statement, witness', analyze

Answer

Q5. An _____ was called out to attend to people involved in a car _____. There were two cars involved and five people were hurt from the _____.

Which one the following combinations of words is the only one which can be inserted into the sentence?

A. ambulance, colision, aciddent

B. ambulance, collision, accidant

C. ambulance, coalision, accidant

D. ambulence, collision, accident

E. ambulance, collision, accident

Answer

Q6. The shop _____ was helping a lady pick out an outfit for a wedding. The woman wanted an outfit that was 'classy, _____ and _____'.

Which one of the following combinations of words is the only one which can be inserted into the sentence?

A. assistant, elegant, feminine

B. asisstant, elegant, feminine

C. assistant, elegent, femininity

D. assistance, ellegent, feminnine

E. assistent, elegant, feminine

Answer

Q7. A postgraduate student decided to go _____ for a year before getting a job. He wanted to _____ different cultures, _____ and ways of living.

Which one of the following combinations of words is the only one which can be inserted into the sentence?

A. travel, experience, lifestyles

B. travelling, experience, lifestyles

C. travels, experiance, lifestyles

D. travelling, experiance, lifestyles

E. travelling, experience, life style

Answer

Q8. A school trip has been _____ for pupils to go to Dover Castle. Teachers _____ not only will it be an experience for the students, but will also help with their _____.

Which one of the following combinations of words is the only one which can be inserted into the sentence?

A. arrange, believe, education

B. aranged, beleive, education

C. arranged, believe, education

D. arranged, beleive, educashion

E. arange, believe, edducation

Answer

Q9. Each _____ firefighter has be at the station within 5 minutes of being called on a _____ pager. This provides a quick and _____ service.

Which one of the following combinations of words is the only one which can be inserted into the sentence?

A. retained, personel, efficiant

B. rettained, personel, efficient

C. retain, personal, eficient

D. retained, personal, efficient

E. retained, personal, efficiant

Answer

Q10. The _____ government had to change its _____ and send another _____ to the Supreme Court.

Which one of the following combinations of words is the only one which can be inserted into the sentence?

A. federal, aproch, propozition

B. federel, approach, proppostion

C. federal, approch, proposishion

D. federel, aproach, proposition

E. federal, approach, proposition

Answer

ANSWERS TO IQ AND APTITUDE TEST SECTION 7 (PART 2)

Q1. D

Q2. A

Q3. C

Q4. D

Q5. E

Q6. A

Q7. B

Q8. C

Q9. D

Q10. E

Now move onto part 3.

IQ AND APTITUDE TEST SECTION 7 (PART 3)

You have 10 minutes to complete part 3.

Q1. Which one of the following sentences is grammatically correct?

A. I wishes you the very best of luck.

B. Our holiday as been postponed.

C. The Government is implementing a new law today.

D. It is difficult to understood my teacher.

Answer [   ]

Q2. Which one of the following sentences is grammatically correct?

A. Please right your name and address on the letter provided.

B. Every day he bring me flowers.

C. Our teacher was of sick today.

D. We are pleased to inform you that you have won a prize.

Answer [   ]

Q3. Which one of the following sentences is grammatically correct?

A. We will be in contact with you shortly.

B. We regret to be in contact with you shortly.

C. Shortly, we will be in contract with you.

D. We will be in contact with you shortley.

Answer [   ]

Q4. Which one of the following sentences is grammatically correct?

A. The queen is bout to give a speech.

B. I get really nervous when I am about to give a speech.

C. Giving speech makes me really nervous.

D. Speaking in front of people makes me nerves.

Answer [   ]

Q5. Which one of the following is grammatically correct?

A. Yours sincerity.

B. Your's sincerely.

C. Yours sincerely.

D. You're sincerely.

Answer [   ]

Q6. Which one of the following sentences is grammatically correct?

A. The president gives speech on national television.

B. We are pleased to inform you that your flight is delayed.

C. We regret to inform you that you have won a holiday.

D. We agree to the terms and conditions.

Answer

Q7. Which one of the following sentences is grammatically correct?

A. Noone likes to be left alone.

B. The lawyer bespoke upon her behalf.

C. The police arrested a man for criminal damage.

D. The train line informed that the train would be delayed.

Answer

Q8. Which one of the following sentences is grammatically correct?

A. The director stopped filming because the actors messed up their lines.

B. The producer were happy for finishing the filming.

C. The acters were doing the best they can.

D. Filming onset can be nervous experience.

Answer

Q9. Which one of the following sentences is grammatically correct?

A. The police has new suspect.

B. The police have a new suspect.

C. The police as a new lead.

D. The police not have any leads to go on.

Answer

Q10. Which one of the following sentences is grammatically correct?

A. We our pleased to inform you that your application was successful.

B. We regret to inform you that you're application was successful.

C. The firefighter service is more than just putting out fires.

D. The ambulance service important role within the medical profession.

Answer

Now check your answers carefully before moving onto part 4.

ANSWERS TO IQ AND APTITUDE TEST SECTION 7 (PART 3)

Q1. C

Q2. D

Q3. A

Q4. B

Q5. C

Q6. D

Q7. C

Q8. A

Q9. B

Q10. C

Now move onto part 4.

IQ AND APTITUDE TEST SECTION 7 (PART 4)

You have 5 minutes to complete part 4.

Q1. Which of the following is not an anagram of types of food?

A. past eight

B. can I roam

C. boar win

D. can peak

E. cool cheat

Answer

Q2. Which of the following is not an anagram of a country?

A. plane

B. chain

C. serial

D. enemy

E. slow

Answer

Q3. Which of the following is not an anagram of sports?

A. loop

B. petals

C. kiss

D. swelter

E. lovely

Answer

Q4. Which of the following is not an anagram of colours?

A. genre

B. sore

C. voile

D. cheap

E. hatred

Answer

Q5. Which of the following is not an anagram of types of trees?

A. hat sere

B. koak cor

C. boules

D. mace roys

E. cut coon

Answer

ANSWERS TO IQ AND APTITUDE TEST SECTION 6 (PART 2)

Q1. C = rainbow

(Spaghetti, macaroni, pancake, chocolate)

Q2. E = owls

(Nepal, China, Israel, Yemen)

Q3. B = pastels

(polo, skis, wrestle, volley)

Q4. E = thread

(green, rose, olive, peach)

Q5. C = blouse

(ash tree, cork oak, sycamore, coconut)

Now move onto part 5.

IQ AND APTITUDE TEST SECTION 7 (PART 5)

You have 20 minutes to complete part 5.

Q1. Start at one of the corner letters and move clockwise around the square finishing in the centre to create a nine-letter word.

A	B	S
T		
C		R

Answer [   ]

Q2. Start at one of the corner letters and move clockwise around the square finishing in the centre to create a nine-letter word.

	M	I
D	S	
	C	A

Answer [   ]

Q3. Start at one of the corner letters and move clockwise around the square finishing in the centre to create a nine-letter word.

U	E	
	S	E
B		L

Answer [   ]

Q4. Start at one of the corner letters and move clockwise around the square finishing in the centre to create a nine-letter word.

S		B
	D	O
G	A	

Answer [   ]

Q5. Start at one of the corner letters and move clockwise around the square finishing in the centre to create a nine-letter word.

S		O
D	M	
	A	S

Answer [   ]

Q6. Start at one of the corner letters and move clockwise around the square finishing in the centre to create a nine-letter word.

	E	A
A		I
L	P	

Answer [   ]

Q7. Start at one of the corner letters and move clockwise around the square finishing in the centre to create a nine-letter word.

N		I
	Y	N
C		D

Answer [   ]

Q8. Start at one of the corner letters and move clockwise around the square finishing in the centre to create a nine-letter word.

I	N	
T	Y	E
		N

Answer [   ]

Q9. Start at one of the corner letters and move clockwise around the square finishing in the centre to create a nine-letter word.

G	N	
A	D	F
M		

Answer [   ]

Q10. Start at one of the corner letters and move clockwise around the square finishing in the centre to create a nine-letter word.

P		
S	R	E
	E	N

Answer [   ]

Q11. Start at one of the corner letters and move clockwise around the square finishing in the centre to create a nine-letter word.

	I	C
P	S	
O	N	

Answer [   ]

Q12. Start at one of the corner letters and move clockwise around the square finishing in the centre to create a nine-letter word.

O	V	
C		R
A		R

Answer [   ]

Q13. Start at one of the corner letters and move clockwise around the square finishing in the centre to create a nine-letter word.

B	L	P
I	E	
	U	A

Answer [   ]

Q14. Start at one of the corner letters and move clockwise around the square finishing in the centre to create a nine-letter word.

R	E	
	T	I
A		S

Answer [   ]

Q15. Start at one of the corner letters and move clockwise around the square finishing in the centre to create a nine-letter word.

S	P	
A		K
M		E

Answer

Now check your answers before moving onto the next section of the guide.

ANSWERS TO IQ AND APTITUDE TEST SECTION 7 (PART 5)

Q1. Abstracts

Q2. Academics

Q3. Bluebells

Q4. Sabotaged

Q5. Sandstorm

Q6. Airplanes

Q7. Indecency

Q8. Intensity

Q9. Magnified

Q10. Newspaper

Q11. Opticians

Q12. Overreact

Q13. Plausible

Q14. Resistant

Q15. Spokesman

Now move onto the next section of the guide.

IQ & APTITUDE TEST
SECTION 8
(General verbal aptitude)

In IQ & Aptitude Test section 8 there are 6 parts.
The time limit for each part is indicated
at the beginning of the test.

IQ AND APTITUDE TEST SECTION 8 (PART 1)

You have 15 minutes to complete part 1.

Q1. Which word does not have a similar meaning to – imaginary?

A. apocryphal

B. fictional

C. illusive

D. inconsistent

Answer

Q2. Which word does not have a similar meaning to – fatigued?

A. enervated

B. exhaustion

C. strength

D. tired

Answer

Q3. Which word does not have a similar meaning to – beautiful?

A. refined

B. grotesque

C. exquisite

D. stunning

Answer

Q4. Which word does not have a similar meaning to – result?

A. outcome

B. effect

C. upshot

D. affect

Answer

Q5. Which word does not have a similar meaning to – important?

A. miniature

B. significant

C. imperative

D. of substance

Answer

Q6. Which word does not have a similar meaning to – conclusion?

A. outcome

B. upshot

C. denouement

D. cause

Answer

[ ]

Q7. Which word does not have a similar meaning to – belittle?

A. criticise

B. downgrade

C. overrate

D. discredit

Answer

[ ]

Q8. Which word does not have a similar meaning to – praise?

A. recognition

B. appreciate

C. plaudit

D. silence

Answer

[ ]

Q9. Which word does not have a similar meaning to – definite?

A. fixed

B. obvious

C. clear-cut

D. vague

Answer

Q10. Which word does not have a similar meaning to – talkative?

A. articulate

B. loquacious

C. affluent

D. voluble

Answer

Q11. Which word does not have a similar meaning to – smart?

A. obtuse

B. resourceful

C. astute

D. adept

Answer

Q12. Which word does not have a similar meaning to – dangerous?

A. treacherous

B. wholesome

C. precarious

D. threatening

Answer

Q13. Which word does not have a similar meaning to – fashionable?

A. shunned

B. style

C. trend

D. hip

Answer

Q14. Which word does not have a similar meaning to – idyllic?

A. ideal

B. picturesque

C. peaceful

D. urban

Answer

[   ]

Q15. Which word does not have a similar meaning to – strange?

A. normal

B. odd

C. peculiar

D. extraordinary

Answer

[   ]

Now check your answers carefully before moving onto part 2.

ANSWERS TO IQ AND APTITUDE TEST SECTION 8 (PART 1)

Q1. D

Q2. C

Q3. B

Q4. D

Q5. A

Q6. D

Q7. C

Q8. D

Q9. D

Q10. C

Q11. A

Q12. B

Q13. A

Q14. D

Q15. A

Now move onto part 2.

IQ AND APTITUDE TEST SECTION 8 (PART 2)

You have 15 minutes to complete part 2.

Q1.Which two words are most opposite in meaning?

Embellished, exaggerated, reduced, standard, overstated, elaborate

Answer

Q2. Which two words are most opposite in meaning?

Frightened, panicked, worried, ecstatic, worried, overrated

Answer

Q3. Which two words are most opposite in meaning?

Peaceful, calm, tranquil, indulge, divert, idyllic

Answer

Q4. Which two words are most opposite in meaning?

Important, famished, significant, noteworthy, momentous, calm

Answer

Q5. Which two words are most opposite in meaning?

Friendly, sociable, welcoming, ignorant, competent, pleasant

Answer

Q6. Which two words are most opposite in meaning?

Imaginary, fictional, unreal, legible, vague

Answer

Q7. Which two words are most opposite in meaning?

Treason, biased, betrayal, disloyalty, honest, sedition

Answer

Q8. Which two words are most opposite in meaning?

Vigorous, exhausted, fatigued, feeble, weary, drained

Answer

Q9. Which two words are most opposite in meaning?

Hatred, sympathy, loathe, callous, animosity, hostility

Answer

Q10. Which two words are most opposite in meaning?

Condemn, affection, love, praise, adore, admire

Answer

Q11. Which two words are most opposite in meaning?

Conclusion, decision, outcome, initiation, result, probability

Answer

Q12. Which two words are most opposite in meaning?

Playful, subdued, submissive, quiet, lethargic, lament

Answer

Q13. Which two words are most opposite in meaning?

Imaginary, realistic, illegible, impracticable, radical, embellished

Answer

Q14. Which two words are most opposite in meaning?

Fantasy, unfeasible, pretend, imagined, reality, fiction

Answer

Q15. Which two words are most opposite in meaning?

Fabrication, misrepresentation, construction, inaccurate, distortion, authenticity

Answer

Now check your answers carefully before moving onto part 3.

ANSWERS TO IQ AND APTITUDE TEST SECTION 8 (PART 2)

Q1. Reduced and standard

Q2. Ecstatic and overrated

Q3. Indulge and divert

Q4. Famished and calm

Q5. Ignorant and competent

Q6. Legible and vague

Q7. Honest and biased

Q8. Vigorous and feeble

Q9. Sympathy and callous

Q10. Condemn and praise

Q11. Initiation and probability

Q12. Playful and lament

Q13. Realistic and impracticable

Q14. Unfeasible and reality

Q15. Inaccurate and authenticity

Now move onto part 3.

IQ AND APTITUDE TEST SECTION 8 (PART 3)

You have 15 minutes to complete part 3.

Q1. Which word is the odd one out?

A. doctor

B. optician

C. nurse

D. surgeon

E. vet

Answer

Q2. Which word is the odd one out?

A. Beef

B. Lamb

C. Cow

D. Pork

E. Chicken

Answer

Q3. Which word is the odd one out?

A. Chare

B. Bench

C. Sofa

D. Bike

E. Bean bag

Answer

Q4. Which word is the odd one out?

A. London

B. Paris

C. Lisbon

D. Prague

E. Nuremberg

Answer

Q5. Which word is the odd one out?

A. Rose

B. Lily

C. Daisy

D. Petal

E. Sunflowers

Answer

Q6. Which word is the odd one out?

A. Bus

B. Train

C. Aeroplane

D. Car

E. Bike

Answer

Q7. Which word is the odd one out?

A. stunning

B. beautiful

C. pretty

D. gorgeous

E. grotesque

Answer

Q8. Which word is the odd one out?

A. anxious

B. affraid

C. terrified

D. fearful

E. aghast

Answer

Q9. Which word is the odd one out?

A. excited

B. eager

C. enthuseastic

D. thrilled

E. stimulated

Answer

Q10. Which word is the odd one out?

A. Strawberries

B. Bananas

C. Grapes

D. Plums

E. Potatoes

Answer

Q11. Which word is the odd one out?

A. Sun

B. Aeroplanes

C. Clouds

D. Birds

E. Tree

Answer

Q12. Which word is the odd one out?

A. hungry

B. ravenous

C. famished

D. esurient

E. stuffed

Answer

Q13. Which word is the odd one out?

A. tired

B. exhausted

C. weeried

D. jaded

E. enervated

Answer

Q14. Which word is the odd one out?

A. Ostrich

B. Parrots

C. Penguins

D. Dodo

E. Owls

Answer

Q15. Which word is the odd one out?

A. Cupboard

B. Table

C. Chairs

D. Door

E. Pillow

Answer

Now check your answers carefully before moving onto part 4.

ANSWERS TO IQ AND APTITUDE TEST SECTION 8 (PART 3)

Q1. E

Q2. C

Q3. A

Q4. E

Q5. D

Q6. E

Q7. E

Q8. B

Q9. C

Q10. E

Q11. E

Q12. E

Q13. C

Q14. D

Q15. E

Now move onto part 4.

IQ AND APTITUDE TEST SECTION 8 (PART 4)

You have 15 minutes to complete part 4.

Q1. Find two words, one from each group, that are closest in meaning:

Group A

Desolate, cold, elated

Group B

Bleak, fervid, beauty

A. desolate and fervid

B. cold and bleak

C. desolate and bleak

D. beauty and elated

Answer

Q2. Find two words, one from each group, that are closest in meaning:

Group A

Loquacious, hot, flower

Group B

Dark, voluble, angry

A. loquacious and voluble

B. loquacious and angry

C. hot and angry

D. flower and voluble

Answer _____

Q3. Find two words, one from each group, that are closest in meaning:

Group A

Angry, tired, playful

Group B

Blissful, fatigued, downfall

A. playful and blissful

B. angry and fatigued

C. angry and downfall

D. tired and fatigued

Answer _____

Q4. Find two words, one from each group, that are closest in meaning:

Group A

Job, lucky, disheartened

Group B

Angry, saddened, university

A. disheartened and saddened

B. disheartened and angry

C. job and university

D. lucky and saddened

Answer [   ]

Q5. Find two words, one from each group, that are closest in meaning:

Group A

Lucky, generous, vulgar

Group B

Uncouth, friendly, leaves

A. generous and uncouth

B. generous and friendly

C. vulgar and uncouth

D. lucky and leaves

Answer [   ]

Q6. Find two words, one from each group, that are closest in meaning:

Group A.

Abysmal, placid, exhausted

Group B

Energetic, docile, wonderful

A. exhausted and docile

B. placid and docile

C. abysmal and docile

D. placid and wonderful

Answer

Q7. Find two words, one from each group, that are closest in meaning:

Group A

Confused, enraged, terrified

Group B

Calm, trance, incensed

A. enraged and incensed

B. confused and calm

C. confused and trance

D. terrified and trance

Answer

```
┌─────────────────────────┐
│                         │
│                         │
│                         │
└─────────────────────────┘
```

Q8. Find two words, one from each group, that are closest in meaning:

Group A

Bewildered, disgusted, fuming

Group B

Happy, indulge, disconcerted

A. fuming and disconcerted

B. disgusted and indulge

C. bewildered and disconcerted

D. disgusted and indulge

Answer

```
┌─────────────────────────┐
│                         │
│                         │
│                         │
└─────────────────────────┘
```

Q9. Find two words, one from each group, that are closest in meaning:

Group A

Idyllic, winter, active

Group B

Lovely, serene, picture

A. idyllic and picture

B. active and lovely

C. idyllic and serene

D. active and picture

Answer
[   ]

Q10. Find two words, one from each group, that are closest in meaning:

Group A

Determined, frightened, informal

Group B

Normal, resolute, unravelling

A. determined and resolute

B. determined and unravelling

C. frightened and unravelling

D. informal and normal

Answer
[   ]

Q11. Find two words, one from each group, that are closest in meaning:

Group A

Gratitude, shy, courageous

Group B

Bold, audacious, friendly

A. shy and friendly

B. gratitude and friendly

C. courageous and audacious

D. gratitude and bold

Answer

Q12. Find two words, one from each group, that are closest in meaning:

Group A

Famished, picturesque, shy

Group B

Happy, introverted, crafty

A. picturesque and happy

B. famished and introverted

C. shy and crafty

D. shy and introverted

Answer

Q13. Find two words, one from each group, that are closest in meaning:

Group A

Hollow, tranquil, hygienic

Group B

Messy, resonating, truth

A. hollow and resonating

B. hollow and messy

C. tranquil and resonating

D. hygienic and messy

Answer

Q14. Find two words, one from each group, that are closest in meaning:

Group A

Cherish, dynamic, treasure

Group B

Appreciate, loud, old

A. dynamic and loud

B. dynamic and old

C. cherish and appreciate

D. treasure and appreciate

Answer

Q15. Find two words, one from each group, that are closest in meaning:

Group A

Tantalising, ferocious, serene

Group B

Behave, enticing, rich

A. ferocious and rich

B. tantalising and enticing

C. serene and enticing

D. serene and rich

Answer

Now check your answers carefully before moving onto the part 5.

ANSWERS TO IQ AND APTITUDE TEST SECTION 8 (PART 4)

Q1. C

Q2. A

Q3. D

Q4. A

Q5. C

Q6. B

Q7. A

Q8. C

Q9. C

Q10. A

Q11. C

Q12. D

Q13. A

Q14. C

Q15. B

Now move onto part 5.

IQ AND APTITUDE TEST SECTION 8 (PART 5)

You have 15 minutes to complete part 5.

Q1.

In the following question you are given two definitions and two words. Place the correct word by each definition.

Noun: the feeling that something is real or true _____

Adjective: that can be accepted as true _____

> *believable, belief*

Q2.

In the following question you are given two definitions and two words. Place the correct word by each definition.

Noun: people who gives disapproval _____

Adjective: looking for faults or problems _____

> *criticism, critical*

Q3.

In the following question you are given two definitions and two words. Place the correct word by each definition.

Noun: to settle an argument/ to choose/ to make up one's mind

_____

Adjective: clear, definite _____

> *decision, decided*

Q4.

In the following question you are given two definitions and two words. Place the correct word by each definition.

Noun: argument _____

Adjective: something that can be questioned or argued about _____

disputable, dispute

Q5.

In the following question you are given two definitions and two words. Place the correct word by each definition.

Noun: a noise, sight, sound preventing concentration _____

Adjective: unable to concentrate properly _____

distraction, distracted

Q6.

In the following question you are given two definitions and two words. Place the correct word by each definition.

Noun: personal respect _____

Adjective: ethical, fair, moral, principled _____

honourable, honour

Q7.

In the following question you are given two definitions and two words. Place the correct word by each definition.

Noun: the ability to create images that are not present _____

Adjective: existing only in the mind _____

imagination, imaginary

Q8.

In the following question you are given two definitions and two words. Place the correct word by each definition.

Noun: annoyance, slight pain _____

Adjective: easily annoyed _____

irritable, irritation

Q9.

In the following question you are given two definitions and two words. Place the correct word by each definition.

Noun: probability _____

Adjective: probably _____

likelihood, likely

Q10.

In the following question you are given two definitions and two words. Place the correct word by each definition.

Noun: art or philosophy of reasoning _____

Adjective: clear, rational, reasonable _____

logic, logical

Q11.

In the following question you are given two definitions and two words. Place the correct word by each definition.

Noun: a sign, advertisement or warning _____

Adjective: attracting attention, easily seen _____

notice, noticeable

Q12.

In the following question you are given two definitions and two words. Place the correct word by each definition.

Noun: act, play, achievement _____

Adjective: doing or acting _____

performing, performance

Q13.

In the following question you are given two definitions and two words. Place the correct word by each definition.

Noun: defence / safety _____

Adjective: trying or intended to protect _____

protection, protective

Q14.

In the following question you are given two definitions and two words. Place the correct word by each definition.

Noun: worthy of respect _____

Adjective: showing consideration or politeness _____

respectful, respectability

Q15.

In the following question you are given two definitions and two words. Place the correct word by each definition.

Noun: pleasure, pride, sense of fulfilment _____

Adjective: acceptable, fair, good enough _____

satisfactory, satisfaction

Now check your answers carefully before moving onto part 6.

IQ AND APTUTUDE TEST SECTION 8 (PART 5)

Q1. Noun – belief, Adjective – believable

Q2. Noun – criticism, Adjective – critical

Q3. Noun – decision, Adjective – decided

Q4. Noun – dispute, Adjective – disputable

Q5. Noun – distraction, Adjective – distracted

Q6. Noun – honour, Adjective – honourable

Q7. Noun – imagination, Adjective – imaginary

Q8. Noun – irritation, Adjective – irritable

Q9. Noun – likelihood, Adjective – likely

Q10. Noun – logic, Adjective – logical

Q11. Noun – notice, Adjective – noticeable

Q12. Noun – performance, Adjective – performing

Q13. Noun – protection, Adjective – protective

Q14. Noun – respectability, Adjective – respectful

Q15. Noun – satisfaction, Adjective – satisfactory

Now move onto part 6.

IQ AND APTITUDE TEST SECTION 8 (PART 6)

You have 10 minutes to complete part 6.

Q1. Which 3 of the 8 three-letter bits can be combined to create a word meaning having been deserted or left?

aba, del, tru, ndo, mne, ned, fli, ing

Answer [   ]

Q2. Which 3 of the 8 three-letter bits can be combined to create a word meaning part of the body that contains all the structures between the chest and the pelvis?

tre, ple, omi, art, abd, wre, ing, nal

Answer [   ]

Q3. Which 3 of the 8 three-letter bits can be combined to create a word meaning a person serving drinks at a bar?

ten, ilu, ing, bar, fri, nig, der, red,

Answer [   ]

Q4. Which 3 of the 8 three-letter bits can be combined to create a word meaning commit treason against or to reveal against one's desire or will?

ray, abd, tru, bet, man, ing, als, pro

Answer

Q5. Which 3 of the 8 three-letter bits can be combined to create a word meaning the action of damaging something or deliberately destroying or obstructing?

ple, ged, rac, sab, art, ota, bre, ing

Answer

Q6. Which 3 of the 8 three-letter bits can be combined to create a word meaning the use of icons to represent something or can be referred to in linguistic terms?

bet, bol, bal, ism, pre, ing, sym, rai

Answer

Q7. Which 3 of the 8 three-letter bits can be combined to create a word meaning cultivating and tending to countryside or as part of horticulture?

ing, est, ima, gar, fen, den, tre, des

Answer

Q8. Which 3 of the 8 three-letter bits can be combined to create a word meaning break the continuity of or interjecting?

qui, bre, err, mis, upt, der, int, ced

Answer
___

Q9. Which 3 of the 8 three-letter bits can be combined to create a word meaning incorrectly positioned or temporarily lost?

ten, pla, tra, mis, als, ing, ced, den

Answer
___

Q10. Which 3 of the 8 three-letter bits can be combined to create a word meaning think about (something) carefully or to deeply consider something?

ada, ten, ing, tra, pon, ism, der, ged

Answer
___

Now check your answers carefully before moving onto the next section of the guide.

ANSWERS TO IQ AND APTITUDE TEST SECTION 8 (PART 6)

Q1. Abandoned

Q2. Abdominal

Q3. Bartender

Q4. Betrayals

Q5. Sabotaged

Q6. Symbolism

Q7. Gardening

Q8. Interrupt

Q9. Misplaced

Q10. Pondering

Now move onto the next section of the guide.

IQ & APTITUDE TEST
SECTION 9
(Abstract and diagrammatic reasoning)

In IQ & Aptitude Test section 9 there are 4 parts.
The time limit for each part is indicated
at the beginning of the test.

IQ AND APTITUDE TEST SECTION 9

You have 10 minutes to complete part 1.

Q1. Which SET does the TEST SHAPE belong to?

SET A	SET B	TEST SHAPE
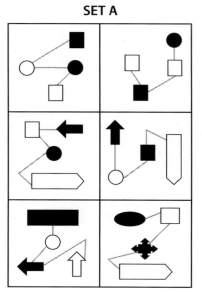	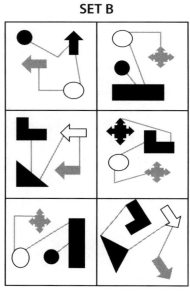	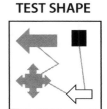

Set A ◯

Set B ◯

Neither ◯

Q2. Which SET does the TEST SHAPE belong to?

SET A	SET B	TEST SHAPE
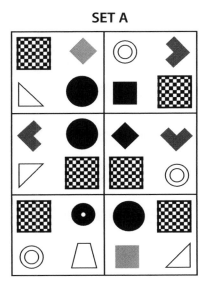	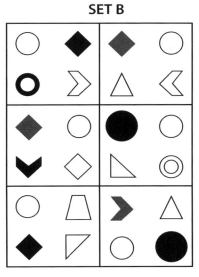	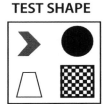

Set A ◯

Set B ◯

Neither ◯

Q3. Which SET does the TEST SHAPE belong to?

SET A

SET B

TEST SHAPE

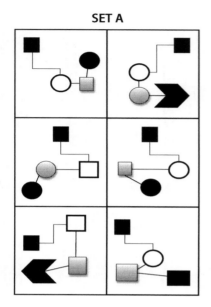

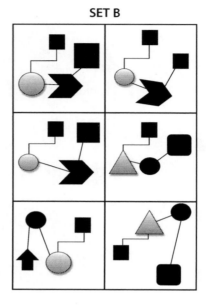

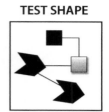

Set A ◯

Set B ◯

Neither ◯

Q4. Which SET does the TEST SHAPE belong to?

SET A	SET B	TEST SHAPE

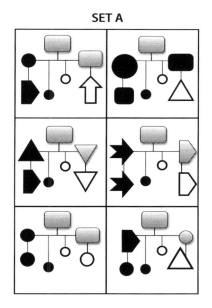 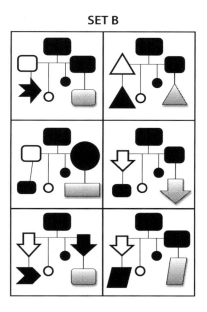 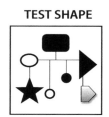

Set A ⬭

Set B ⬭

Neither ⬭

Q5. Which SET does the TEST SHAPE belong to?

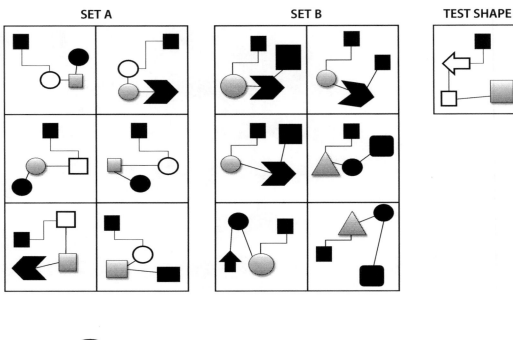

Set A ◯

Set B ◯

Neither ◯

Now check your answers carefully before moving onto part 2.

ANSWERS TO IQ AND APTITUDE TEST SECTION 9 (PART 1)

Q1. Neither

Explanation: The test shape does not fit in to either Sets. It does not fit in to either sets because the test shape has two grey shapes, which does not follow the pattern in either set.

Q2. Set A

Explanation: The test shape fits in to Set A. This is because in set A each square contains a black shape, a white shape, a chequered shape and a grey shape. This is apparent in the Test shape and therefore belongs to this set.

Q3. Set B

Explanation: The test shape fits in to Set B. Set B starts with a black shape, which is linked to a grey shape, to a black shape, to a black shape. The Test shape follows this pattern and therefore belongs to this set.

Q4. Set B

Explanation: The test shape fits in to set B. Set B starts with a black shape. The row below then follows the sequence white and black. The bottom line follows the sequence black, white, black and grey. Therefore the test shape follows set B.

Q5. Neither

Explanation: The test shape does not belong to either Sets. It is clear that the test shape contains two white shapes. Neither of the sets follows this pattern and therefore cannot belong to either set.

Now move onto part 2.

IQ AND APTITUDE TEST SECTION 9

You have 10 minutes to complete part 2.

Q1. Which figure comes next in the series?

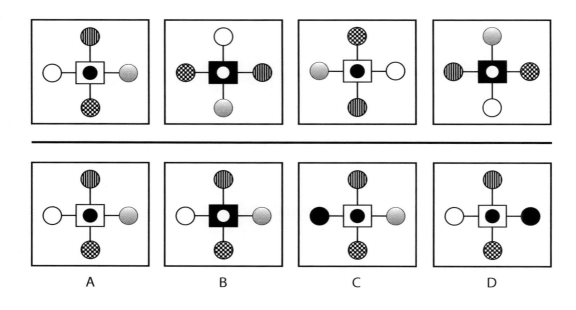

A

B

C

D

Neither

Q2. Which figure comes next in the series?

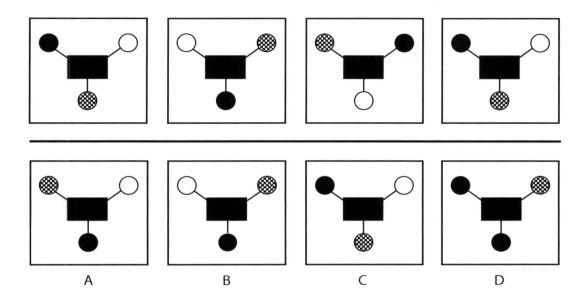

A ◯

B ◯

C ◯

D ◯

Neither ◯

Q3. Which figure comes next in the series?

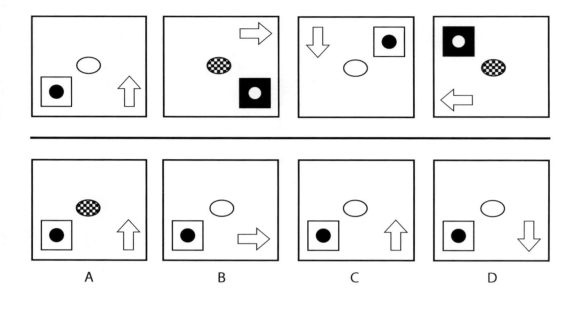

A

B

C

D

A ◯

B ◯

C ◯

D ◯

Neither ◯

Q4. Which figure comes next in the series?

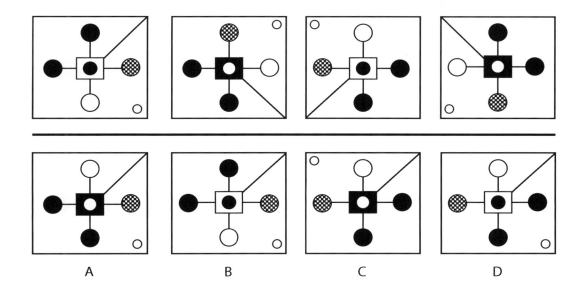

A
B
C
D

A ◯

B ◯

C ◯

D ◯

Neither ◯

Q5. Which figure comes next in the series?

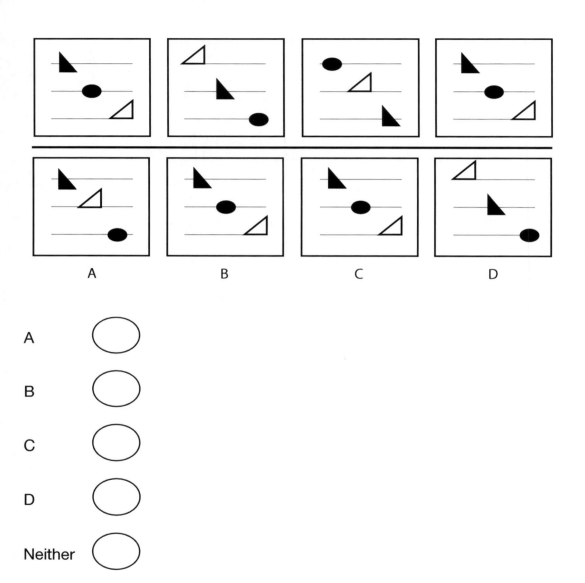

A ◯

B ◯

C ◯

D ◯

Neither ◯

Now check your answers carefully before moving onto part 3.

ANSWERS TO IQ AND APTITUDE TEST SECTION 9 (PART 2)

Q1. A

Explanation: The four outer circles are rotated clockwise. The rectangle and inner circle alternate colours from white to black, to black to white. So, the next figure in the sequence needs to be a white square, with a black inner circle, and the circles need to be rotated 90 degrees clockwise.

Q2. B

Explanation: The middle rectangle stays in the same position throughout the sequence. The circles move in an anti-clockwise motion throughout the sequence.

Q3. C

Explanation: Within each square the shapes are all moving round in an anti-clockwise manner as the sequence progresses. The inner circle is alternating between white and chequered. The square and small inner circle are alternating between black and white as the sequence progresses. The arrow within each square is moving clockwise as the sequence progresses.

Q4. B

Explanation: Within each square the shapes are moving round clockwise as the sequence progresses. You will notice that the square and inner circle which form the centre of each shape are each alternating between black and white as the sequence progresses. The diagonal line within each square is moving round clockwise as the sequence progresses. The small white dot in the corner of each square is moving round anti-clockwise as the sequence progresses.

Q5. D

Explanation: Within each square the shapes are moving down each line as the sequence progresses. Once they reach the bottom they go back to the top.

Now move onto part 3.

IQ AND APTITUDE TEST SECTION 9 (PART 3)

You have 10 minutes to complete part 3.

Q1.

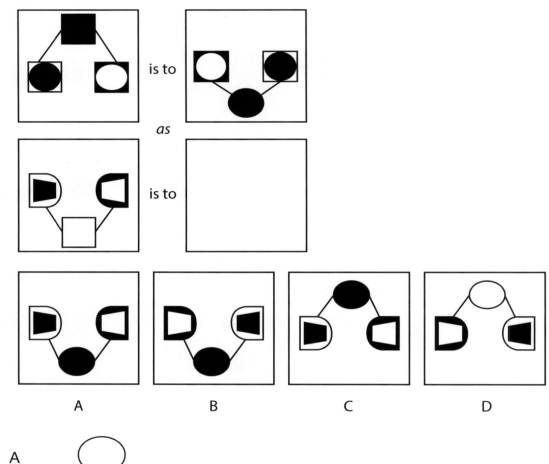

A 〇

B 〇

C 〇

D 〇

Neither 〇

Q2.

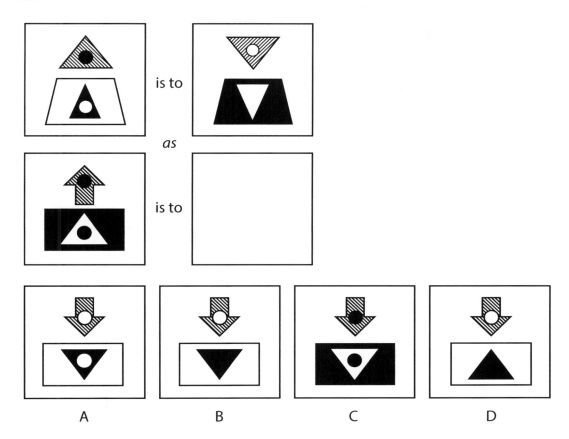

A

B

C

D

A ◯

B ◯

C ◯

D ◯

Neither ◯

Q3.

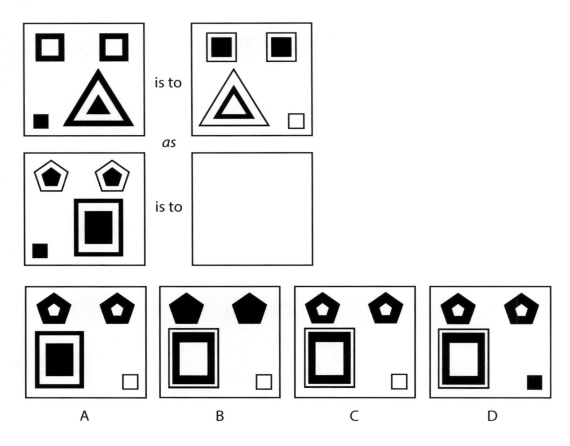

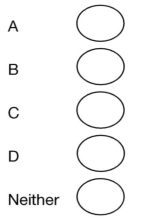

A

B

C

D

Neither

Q4.

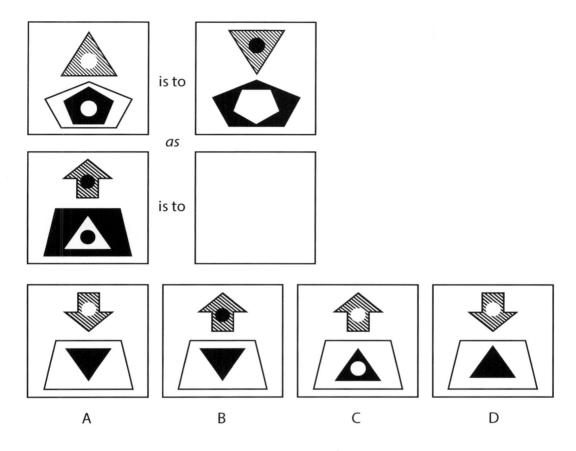

A

B

C

D

Neither

Q5.

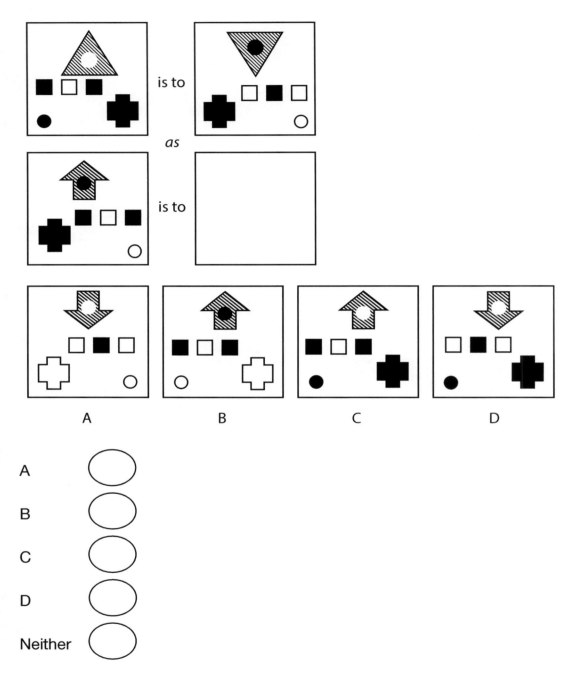

A ⃝

B ⃝

C ⃝

D ⃝

Neither ⃝

Now check your answers carefully before moving onto part 4.

ANSWERS TO IQ AND APTITUDE TEST SECTION 9 (PART 3)

Q1. D

Explanation: Within the first diagram, the black square moves to the bottom and is replaced by a circle. The colour format for the first diagram is a white square with a black circle. The second square is a black square with a white circle. This transforms into opposites in the following diagram. The first square is now a black square with a white circle and the second square is now a white square with a black circle.

So, the diagram you are trying to work out has to follow this format. The white square at the bottom will turn into a white circle at the top of the next diagram. The colour pattern is exactly the same as above, so option D gives you the same format.

Q2. B

Explanation: In the top left square there is a striped triangle with a black circle in the centre. Below this is a white trapezium with black triangle with a white circle. In the top right hand square the striped triangle is now inverted and the circle is black. Below this the trapezium is now black, the inner triangle inverted and white with no central circle.

Q3. C

Explanation: Within the first diagram, the top black squares have an inner white square, which in the next square becomes a white square with a black inner square. The triangle alternates between black, white and black which is alternated in the next diagram to be white, black, white. In the bottom left corner, there is a black rectangle which changes to a white rectangle at the bottom right corner.

So, the diagram you are trying to work out has to follow this format. The pentagon is white with a black inner pentagon, so in the next diagram is needs to be a black pentagon with a white inner pentagon. The rectangles alternating between black, white and black need to be changed in reverse (white, black, white). In the left hand corner, there is a black square, so that needs to be replaced with a white square and placed at the bottom right corner.

Q4. A

Explanation: Within the first diagram there is a striped triangle with a white circle. This is 'as to' a striped triangle facing downwards with a black circle. The white pentagon contains a smaller black pentagon and a white dot. In the next diagram, it shows a black pentagon, with an inner white pentagon facing downwards, and the dot has been removed.

So, the diagram you are trying to work out has to follow this format. The striped arrow with the black dot will be a striped arrow pointing downwards with a white dot. The black trapezium shape with an inner white triangle and black dot will be replaced with a white trapezium, with a black triangle pointing downwards, with the dot being removed.

Q5. D

Explanation: within the first diagram, there is a striped triangle with a white inner circle. This changes to a striped downward pointing triangle with a black inner circle. The black cross in the bottom right corner, changes to a black cross in the bottom left corner. The black dot in the bottom left corner changes to a white dot in the bottom right corner. Three horizontal squares are placed in the middle, slightly to the left with the colour pattern black, white, black. This changes to the squares being moved in the middle slightly to the right and have the colour pattern white, black, white.

So, the diagram you are trying to work out has to follow this format. The striped arrow with the black inner dot becomes a striped downwards pointing arrow with a white inner dot. The cross moves from the left hand side, to the right hand side but remains the same colour. The white dot at the bottom right corner becomes a black dot in the bottom left corner. The horizontal squares move from the middle, slightly to the left with the colour pattern black, white, black to being slightly to the right and have the colour pattern white, black, white.

Now move onto part 4.

IQ AND APTITUDE TEST SECTION 9 (PART 4)

You have 10 minutes to complete part 4.

Q1. Which figure comes next in the sequence?

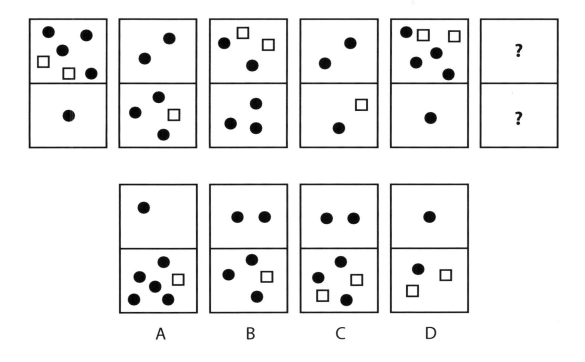

A ◯

B ◯

C ◯

D ◯

Q2. Which figure comes next in the sequence?

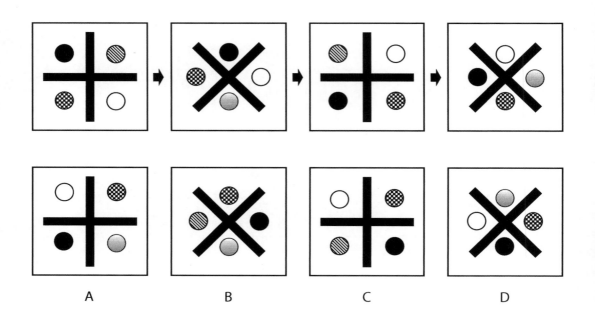

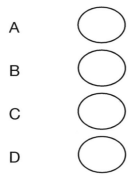

A

B

C

D

Q3. Which figure comes next in the sequence?

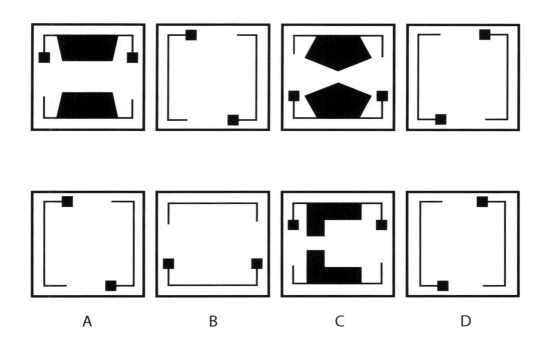

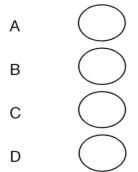

A ◯

B ◯

C ◯

D ◯

Q4. Which figure comes next in the sequence?

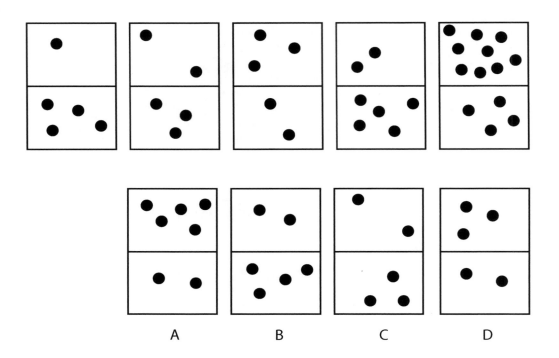

A

B

C

D

Q5. Which figure comes next in the sequence?

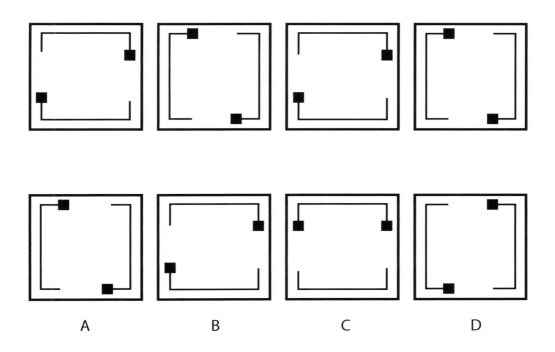

A   B   C   D

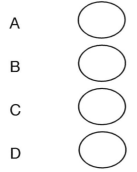

A

B

C

D

ANSWERS TO IQ AND APTITUDE TEST SECTION 9 (PART 4)

Q1. B

Explanation: The number of dots starts off as 4 in the top of the first rectangle and 1 in the bottom. The number of squares in the top of the first rectangle is 2 and 0 in the bottom. As the sequence progresses, you will notice that from looking at the alternate sections of the rectangles (starting from the top of the first rectangle), the dots decrease by 1 each time, once it gets to 1, the pattern starts again with 4 dots. The white squares alternate between 2 and 1 in the same section of the rectangle.

From starting at the bottom of the first rectangle, you will notice there is one dot, the pattern in alternating sections of each rectangle adds one dot each time until it reaches 3. It then works from 3 back down to 1.

Q2. C

Explanation: The sequence alternates between a plus sign and a cross sign, each with circular shapes moving around the signs in an anti-clockwise manner.

Q3. C

Explanation: The sequence alternates between solid black shapes inside horizontal 'brackets' and vertical brackets with a black square at one end of each bracket. Therefore, the correct answer is D as this is the only option that is similar to shapes 1 and 3 in the sequence.

Q4. C

Explanation: The number of dots starts off as an odd number (1) in top of the first rectangle and an even number (4) in the bottom. As the sequence progresses the number of dots in the alternate section of the next rectangle in the sequence remains either odd or even.

Q5. B

Explanation: The pattern is rotating in an anti-clockwise manner. So, the next figure in the sequence will be the same as figures 1 and 3 in the sequence because, once it is rotated, the brackets become horizontal and not vertical, it will go back to same position.

A FEW FINAL WORDS

You have now reached the end of the testing guide and no doubt you will be ready to take your assessment. The majority of candidates who pass their test have a number of common attributes. These are as follows:

1. They believe in themselves.

The first factor is self-belief. Regardless of what anyone tells you, you can pass your test or assessment and secure your chosen job. Just like any selection test, you have to be prepared to work hard in order to be successful. Make sure you have the self-belief to pass the selection process and fill your mind with positive thoughts.

2. They prepare fully.

The second factor is preparation. Those people who achieve in life prepare fully for every eventuality and that is what you must do when you apply for any job or promotion. Work very hard and especially concentrate on your weak areas.

3. They persevere.

Perseverance is a fantastic word. Everybody comes across obstacles or setbacks in their life, but it is what you do about those setbacks that is important. If you fail at something, then ask yourself 'why' you have failed. This will allow you to improve for next time and if you keep improving and trying, success will eventually follow. Apply this same method of thinking when you prepare for your IQ and aptitude test.

4. They are self-motivated.

How much do you want this job? Do you want it, or do you really want it?

When you apply for any job you should want it more than anything in the world. Your levels of self-motivation will shine through on your application and during your interview. For the weeks and months leading up to the selection process, be motivated as best you can and always keep your fitness levels up as this will serve to increase your levels of enthusiasm and concentration.

Work hard, stay focused and be what you want…

Richard McMunn

P.S. Don't forget, you can get FREE access to more tests online at:

www.PsychometricTestsOnline.co.uk

**Get more career
testing and interview books at:**

www.How2Become.com

Printed in Great Britain
by Amazon